Andreas Spreinat

Malawisee-Cichliden • Cichlids from Lake Malawi

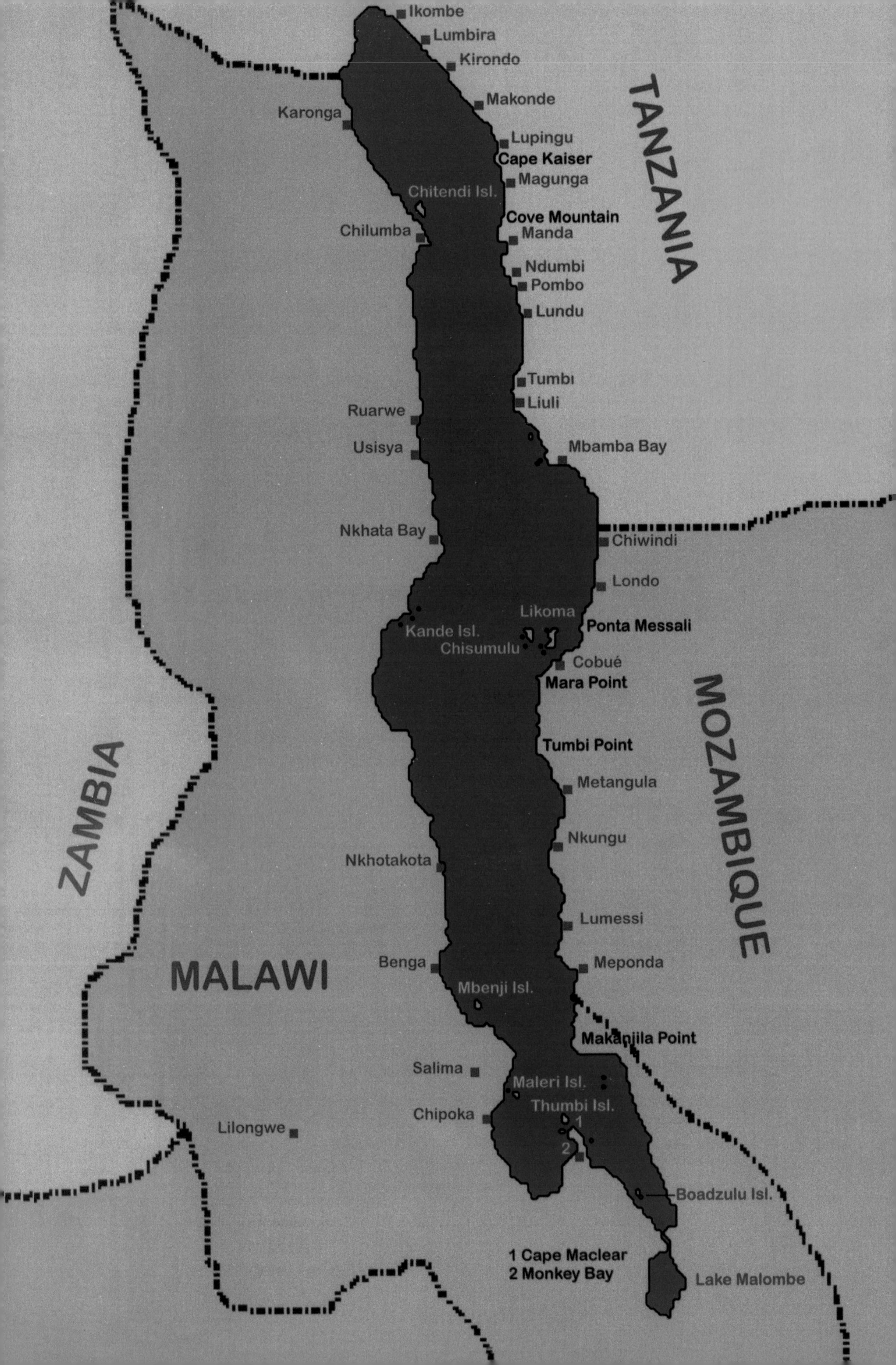

TANZANIA
ZAMBIA
MALAWI
MOZAMBIQUE
Ikombe
Lumbira
Kirondo
Makonde
Karonga
Lupingu
Cape Kaiser
Magunga
Chitendi Isl.
Cove Mountain
Chilumba
Manda
Ndumbi
Pombo
Lundu
Tumbi
Liuli
Ruarwe
Usisya
Mbamba Bay
Nkhata Bay
Chiwindi
Londo
Likoma
Ponta Messali
Kande Isl.
Chisumulu
Cobué
Mara Point
Tumbi Point
Metangula
Nkungu
Nkhotakota
Lumessi
Benga
Meponda
Mbenji Isl.
Makanjila Point
Salima
Maleri Isl.
Thumbi Isl.
Chipoka
Lilongwe
1
2
Boadzulu Isl.
1 Cape Maclear
2 Monkey Bay
Lake Malombe

Aqualex-catalog

Andreas Spreinat

Malawisee-Cichliden
Cichlids from Lake Malawi

Dähne Verlag

Die Deutsche Bibliothek –
CIP-Einheitsaufnahme

Ein Titeldatensatz für diese
Publikation ist bei der
Deutschen Bibliothek erhältlich

Aqualex-catalog

Andreas Spreinat
Malawisee-Cichliden
Cichlids from Lake Malawi

2., aktualisierte und erweiterte Auflage 2002
ISBN 3-921684-49-8

©1997 Dähne Verlag GmbH, Postfach 250, D-76256 Ettlingen

Alle Rechte liegen beim Verlag.
Das gesamte Werk ist urheberrechtlich geschützt. Jede Verwertung außerhalb der Grenzen des Urheberrechtsgesetzes
ist ohne Zustimmung des Verlages unzulässig und strafbar. Das gilt insbesondere für Vervielfältigungen, Nachdruck,
die Verbreitung durch Bild, Funk, Fernsehen und Internet, durch fotomechanische Wiedergabe und Datenverarbeitungssysteme
sowie für Übersetzungen.
Alle Angaben in diesem Buch sind sorgfältig geprüft und geben den neuesten Wissensstand wieder.
Eine Garantie kann dennoch nicht übernommen werden. Eine Haftung des Verfassers oder des Verlages
für Personen-, Sach- oder Vermögensschäden ist ausgeschlossen.

All rights reserved.
No part of this publication may be reproduced or transmitted in any form or by any means without permission.

Herstellung: Werner Trauthwein
Lithos: HWD M. Vogel, Karlsruhe
Druck: Kraft-Druck, Ettlingen

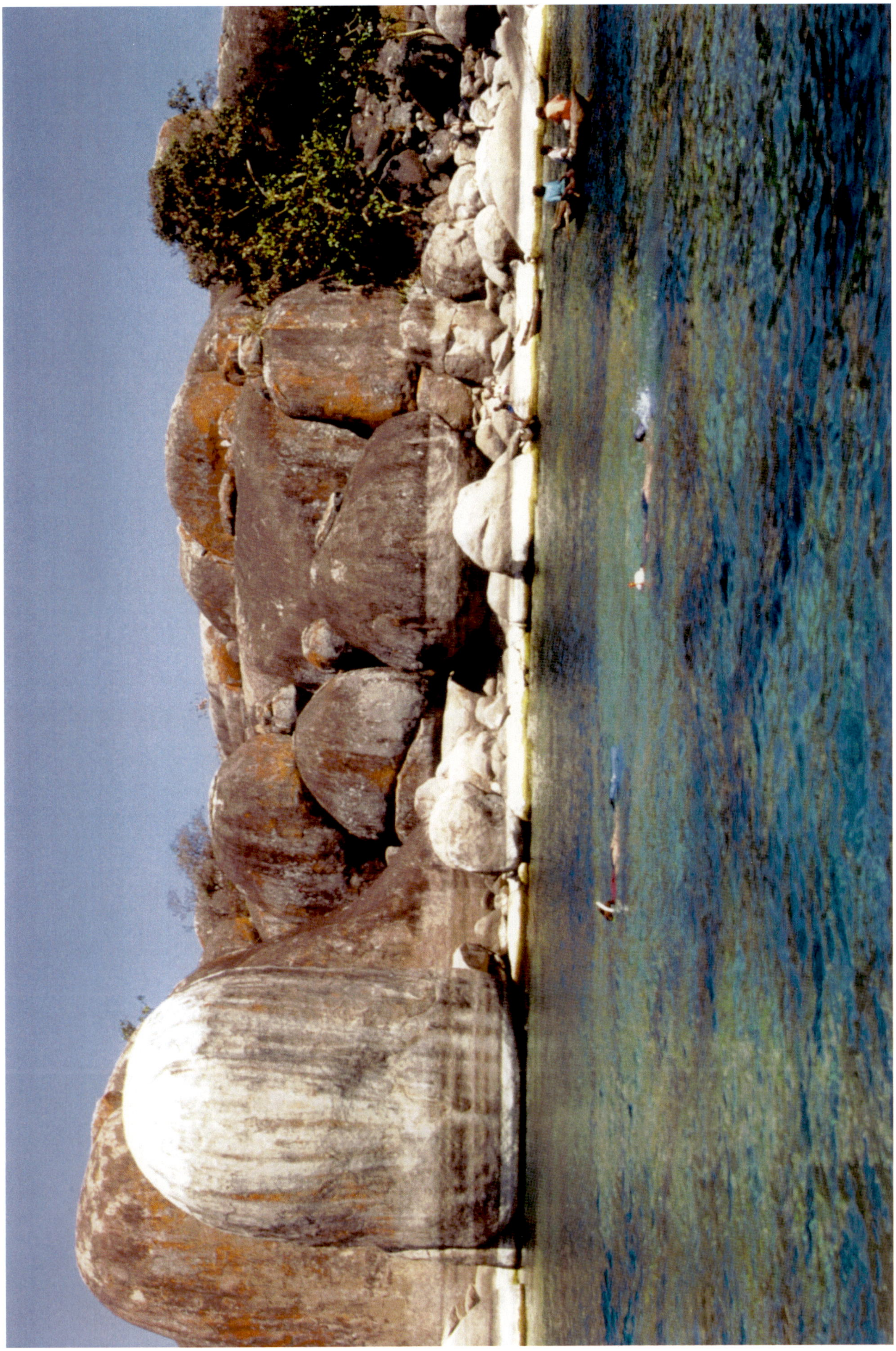

Vorwort und Danksagung

Es ist über 30 Jahre her, daß die ersten lebenden Buntbarsche des Malawisees eingeführt worden sind. Die Aquarianer waren seinerzeit so begeistert von der ungewöhnlichen Farbenpracht der neuen Arten, daß in den Fachzeitschriften überschwänglich von den „Korallenfischen des Süßwassers," berichtet wurde. Stolze Preise wurden Anfang der 1960er Jahre für die ersten Wildfänge bezahlt. Das änderte sich zunehmend, als man feststellte, wie einfach diese im weiblichen Geschlecht maulbrütenden Cichliden zu züchten sind. Preiswerte Nachzuchttiere fanden sich deshalb wenig später bereits im Sortiment des Zoofachhandels, so daß man sich auch mit schmalerem Geldbeutel diesen schönen Cichliden zuwenden konnte.

Obwohl mittlerweile seit mehr als 30 Jahren eine Vielzahl von neuen, auch der Wissenschaft völlig unbekannten Arten von kommerziellen Exporteuren gefangen und in alle Welt verschickt worden ist, – der Reigen an neuen Arten und Farbvarianten ist keineswegs zum Stillstand gekommen. Malawisee-Cichliden zählen nach wie vor zu den beliebtesten Buntbarschen. Eine Anzahl aquaristischer Fachbücher über Malawisee-Cichliden ist erschienen, in denen teilweise detailliert über die verschiedenen Arten berichtet wird. Bemerkenswerterweise fehlte bislang aber ein Buch, welches die wichtigsten Arten in übersichtlicher Form zusammenfaßt, so dass auch dem weniger spezialisierten Aquarianer eine Orientierung ermöglicht wird. Der Verfasser hat deshalb den Vorschlag des Dähne Verlags gerne angenommen und die Gelegenheit genutzt, diese „Lücke", zu schließen. Besonders freut es mich als Autor, daß die nun in Katalogform vorliegende Zusammenfassung der bislang bekannten Malawisee-Cichlidenarten zu einem günstigen Preis realisiert werden konnte. Dafür und für die entgegenkommende, angenehme Zusammenarbeit danke ich dem Dähne Verlag.

Manchem Leser könnte der Informationsgehalt auf den nachfolgenden Bildseiten als zu gering erscheinen. Doch der Aqualex Malawisee-Cichliden-Katalog ist nicht isoliert zu sehen. Der Hintergrund für die Veröffentlichung des vorliegenden Kataloges ist die Multimedia-CD-ROM „Aqualex Malawisee-Cichliden,", deren Programmierung in vorbildlicher Weise von Lutz Döring, Echte Software, und seinem Sohn Karsten vorgenommen wurde, wofür den beiden mein Dank und meine Anerkennung gebührt. Auf dieser CD-ROM werden erstmals die wichtigsten Informationen über Malawisee-Buntbarsche in elektronischer Form zusammengefaßt. Neben den mehr als 2000 Farbbildern und ausführlichen Videosequenzen bietet die CD-ROM alle Vorteile eines modernen Computerprogramms, angefangen von der Möglichkeit des Ergänzens und Aktualisierens der zusammengetragenen Informationen über Suchfunktionen bis zum Einfügen eigener Bilder durch den Anwender. Quasi als „Auskopplung", aus der CD-ROM faßt der Katalog die wichtigsten Arten in kompakter Form zusammen und ermöglicht dem Aquanianer eine praxisbezogene, rasche Übersicht über diese so komplexe Fischgruppe.

Danken möchte ich an dieser Stelle auch den vielen Aquarianerkollegen, die mir mit Rat und Tat zur Seite standen oder mir ihre Fische zum Fotografieren zur Verfügung stellten. Insbesondere erwähnen möchte ich hier Friedrich Staats, Bremke; Walter Sievers, Tündern; Edwin Reitz (Aquaport), Hannover; Erwin Bressmer, Weilheim/Teck; Peter Bär und Erwin Hartmann, Obergünzburg; Peter Enge, Bielefeld; Katrin Tebbe, Schieder; Peter Baasch, Stegen; Reinhold Müller, Frankfurt; Markus Schlangen (Malawi-Tanganjika-Aquarium), Neuss; Thomas Lepel und Marc Danhieux (Mal-Ta-Vi), Hohenahr-Erda; Helmut Löfflad (Cichlidenstadl), Alerheim-Bühl sowie Klaus-Dieter Nentwich (Cichlid Aquaristik), Kaufbeuren.

Besonderer Dank gebührt den Menschen „vor Ort,", die mich während meiner Exkursionen an diesen faszinierenden See maßgeblich unterstützt haben. Erling Johansen, Mbeya/ Tansania; Stuart Grant, Salima/Malawi aber auch seinerzeit Norman Edwards, Monkey Bay/Malawi, wie in gleicher Weise selbstverständlich den jeweiligen dazugehörigen Teams möchte ich meinen herzlichen Dank aussprechen.

Und natürlich möchte ich nicht versäumen, auch meiner Frau Kerstin für ihr Verständnis zu danken, daß sie (wieder einmal) viele Urlaubstage (und Nächte) ohne mich verbrachte, derweil ich die Dias, Daten und Texte für das vorliegende Buch und die CD-ROM zusammengestellt habe. Sie hat mich dazu ermutigt, diese Arbeit aufzunehmen, so dass sie letztlich den größten Anteil daran hat.

Trotz aller Sorgfalt und Mühe, die ich gleichermaßen sowohl für den Katalog als auch für die CD-ROM aufgewandt habe, ist mir völlig klar, daß Fehler und Unkorrektheiten enthalten sein werden. Es ist mir deshalb ein besonderes Anliegen, die Erfarungen und Kenntnisse der Leser kennenzulernen, jeder Hinweis und jede Anregung sind mir ganz besonders willkommen.

Göttingen, im August 1996

Andreas Spreinat

Foreword and Acknowledgements

It is over 30 years since the first living cichlids from Lake Malawi were imported. The aquarists at that time were so enthusiastic about the unusual coloration of these riew species that they referred to them as "Fresh Water Goral fish" in the ornamental fish journals. Enormous prices were paid at the beginning of the 1960s for the first wild-caught fish. This situation gradually changed as it became apparent how easy it is to breed these maternal mouthbrooding cichlids and inexpensive captive-bred fish soon became available in the assortment offered by the specialist ornamental fish trade.

Although new, scientifically unknown species have been caught by commercial exporters and sent throughout the world for more than 30 years, the sequence of new species and colour forms has still not come to a halt. Lake Malawi cichlids are still some of the most well-loved cichlids. A number of aquaristic books on the Lake Malawi cichlids have been published, in which there have been detailed reports about some of the species. Remarkably as yet, no book has been written which summarises the most important species in an easily surveyed form that would even provide an orientation for the less specialised aquarists. The author was therefore happy to accept the suggestion of the German publishing house of Dähne Verlag to fill this "gap". It pleases me especially as the author that a summary of the known Lake Malawi cichlids could he catlogued and made available at a reasonable price. I wish to thank Dähne Verlag for this opportunity and for the collegial and enjoyable collaboration.

The amount of information presented in the following pages may appear as being too small to some readers, but the Aqualex Lake Malawi Cichlid Catalogue is not to be considered in isolation. The basis for the publication of this catalogue is the Multimedia-CD-ROM "Aqualex Lake Malawi Cichlids". This has been a exemplary programmed by Lutz Döring, Echte Software, Germany and his son Karsten, for which they both deserve my acknowledgement and appreciation. On this CD-ROM for the first time the most important information concerning the Lake Malawi cichlids has been summarised in an electronic form. Along with more than 1 500 colour photographs and numerous video sequences, this CD-ROM offers all the advantages of a modern Computer program – the possibility of the amendment and actualisation of the compiled data, search functions and the possibility for the user to insert their own picturcs. The catalogue being quasi a selection of the data from the CD-ROM, presents the most important species in a compact form thereby making it possible for the aquarist to have a practical, quick over-view of this extremely complex group of fish.

I also wish to thank at this point the numerons fellow aquarists who have provided me with both advice and practical help or who have permitted me to photograph their fish. I wish to especially thank Friedrich Staats, Bremke, Walter Sievers, Tündern, Edwin Reitz (Aquapport), Hannover, Germany; Erwin Bressmer, Weilheim/Teck, Germany; Peter Bär and Erwin Hartmann, Obergünzburg, Germany; Peter Enge, Bielefeld, Germany; Katrin Tebbe, Schieder, Germany; Peter Baasch, Stegen, Germany; Reinhold Müller, Frankfurt, Germany; Markus Schlangen (Malawi-Tanganjika-Aquarium), Neuß, Germany; Thomas Lepel and Marc Danhieux (Maltavi), Hohenahr-Erda, Germany; Helmut Löfflad (Cichlidenstadel), Alerheim-Bühl, Germany and Klaus-Dieter Nentwich (Cichlid Aquaristik), Kaufbeuren, Germany.

An especial thanks has been warranted by the people "in situ" who provided considerable support during my excursions to this fascinating lake. I wish to extend my heartfelt thanks to Erling Johansen, Mbeya, Tanzania; Stuart Grant, Salima, Malawi and also to Norman Edwards, Monkey Bay, Malawi, for his help while he worked on the lake, as well as to their respective teams.

And naturally, I do not wish to forget to thank my wife Kerstin for her understanding that (yet again) she has spent many holidays (and nights) without me as I was too busy amalgamating the slides, data and texts for this book and CD-ROM. She encouraged me to start this work and so she really deserves the lion's share of my appreciation and thanks.

Despite all the care and attention which I have employed in producing the catalogue and CD-ROM, I am quite certain that they will still contain mistakes and inaccuracies. It is therefore most important for me to become acquainted with the experience and knowledge of the reader. Every suggestion and piece of relevant information will be greatly welcomed.

Göttingen, August 1996

Andreas Spreinat

Der See

Der Malawisee, früher Njassasee genannt, befindet sich im südlichen Ende des ostafrikanischen Grabenbruchsystems. Die Nord-Süd-Ausdehnung beträgt fast 600 km bei einer maximalen Breite von etwa 80 km. Seine Fläche wird mit nahezu 31 000 Quadratkilometern angegeben, die maximale Tiefe liegt bei über 700 Metern. Damit ist der Malawisee nach dem Viktoria- und Tanganjikasee der drittgrößte See Afrikas.

Drei Anrainerstaaten begrenzen dieses Binnenmeer. Den größten Anteil Küstenlinie weist Malawi auf. Fast die gesamte Westküste sowie ein Teil des südlichen bis mittleren Ostufers gehören zu diesem Staat, was ungefähr 800 km Küste entspricht. Mosambik grenzt an etwa 200 km der mittleren Ostküste. Die Nordostküste sowie ein vernachlässigbar kleiner Bereich der nördlichen Westküste zählen zu Tansania; dies macht rund weitere 300 km Küstenlinie aus. In Tansania wie auch in Mosambik wird dieser See übrigens auch heute noch Njassasee (engl. Lake Nyasa) genannt, was in der Sprache der Yao „großes Wasser" bedeutet.

Der Malawisee ist ein wahrlich einmaliges Gewässer. Wenn man an den zum Teil weitläufigen Sandstränden ein Bad in der Brandung nimmt, ist man geradezu überrascht, dass das Wasser nicht salzig schmeckt. Neben den langen, flachen Sandstränden gibt es überwiegend steinige und felsige Uferbereiche, an denen insbesondere die als „Mbunas" bekannten Felsencichliden vorkommen. Weite Flussmündungen sowie sumpfige und mit Schilf bestandene Ufer runden das abwechselungsreiche Bild des Malawisees ab. Erwähnenswert sind hier weiterhin die gewaltigen Bergketten, die den See an der Nordwestküste (nördlich von Nkhata Bay) sowie vor allem an der Nordostküste mit dem Livingstone Gebirge förmlich einrahmen und so den Grabenbruch, durch den der Malawisee vor schätzungsweise 1-2 Millionen Jahren entstanden ist, eindrucksvoll verdeutlichen.

Es besteht kein Zweifel darüber, dass die größte Besonderheit des Malawisees die Buntbarsche darstellen. Mittlerweile dürften wohl mehr als 600 Arten bekannt sein, viele davon sind aber wissenschaftlich noch unbeschrieben und werden unter sogenannten Arbeitsnamen und Handelsbezeichnungen geführt (s. u.). Bis auf ganz wenige Ausnahmen leben alle Cichliden endemisch im Malawisee, d. h., sie kommen nur in diesem Gewässer vor und sonst nirgends auf der Welt.

Die Cichliden des Malawisees

Grundsätzlich lassen sich zwei große Gruppen von Malawisee-Cichliden unterscheiden: Mbunas und Nicht-Mbunas. Als Mbunas werden von den Einheimischen die sogenannten Felsencichliden bezeichnet. Hierunter versteht man eine in sich weitgehend geschlossene, d. h., gegenüber anderen Buntbarschen gut abgrenzbare, Einheit von kleinen bis mittelgroßen Cichliden, die mit wenigen Ausnahmen eine strikt felsorientierte Lebensweise besitzen. Die Nahrungsgrundlage der Mbunas bildet der Felsaufwuchs, der mit Hilfe unterschiedlicher Techniken abgeschabt, abgezupft oder durchkämmt wird. Dabei ist zu berücksichtigen, dass Felsaufwuchs, oder generell der auf Hartsubstraten sich ansiedelnde Aufwuchs, zwar überwiegend aus Algen und Bakterien besteht, aber dennoch eine Vielzahl von Kleintieren enthält (z. B. Insektenlarven, Krebschen, kleine Würmer und Schnecken). Es liegt auf der Hand, dass der Aufwuchs insbesondere da gut gedeiht, wo viel Sonnenenergie zur Verfügung steht, also im flachen Wasser bis etwa 5 Meter Tiefe. Dies dürfte der Hauptgrund dafür sein, dass die meisten Mbunas im flachen Wasser vorkommen. Im extrem Flachwasser (bis etwa 1 m Tiefe) leben übrigens die besonders kräftigen bzw. durchsetzungsfähigsten Arten, die ihre Nahrungskonkurrenten in tiefere und damit nahrungsärmere Wasserbereiche abdrängen. Obwohl viele Arten spezielle Aufwuchs-Fresstechniken entwickelt haben, werden andere Nahrungsquellen, insbesondere wenn diese leicht verfügbar sind, keineswegs verschmäht. Bei entsprechendem Aufkommen von Plankton kann man die Mbunas in großen Gruppen im freien Wasser beim Fressen beobachten; für manche Arten stellt Plankton dann die Hauptnahrung dar.

Zur Zeit werden die Mbunas in 12 Gattungen eingeteilt: *Cyathochromis, Cynotilapia, Genyochromis, Gephyrochromis, Iodotropheus, Labeotropheus, Labidochromis, Melanochromis, Maylandia, Petrotilapia, Pseudotropheus* und *Tropheops*. Insgesamt dürften es wohl fast 300 Arten sein, die mittlerweile bekannt sind. Bei einigen Populationen konnte bislang nicht eindeutig geklärt werden, ob es sich um geographische Rassen bereits bekannter Arten oder um neue eigenständige Arten handelt, so dass man zur Zeit keine exakte Artenzahl nennen kann. Die kleinsten Mbunas werden nur etwa 6-7 cm groß (Gesamtlänge). Die größten Mbunas sind die Vertreter der Gattung *Petrotilapia*, die im männlichen Geschlecht durchaus 18 cm Gesamtlänge erreichen können. Die Mehrheit der Mbunas liegt aber im Größenbereich von 9-11 cm.

Die enge Bindung der Mbunas an felsige Untergründe führt dazu, dass die meisten Arten sehr standorttreu sind. Weiterhin ist von Bedeutung, dass selbst kleine, nur 20 Meter breite sandige Bereiche von vielen Mbunas nicht überschwommen werden. Auf diese Weise existieren viele isolierte Populationen, die sich im Laufe der Zeit verschieden entwickelt und zum Beispiel farblich unterschiedliche Standortvarianten gebildet haben. Letztlich führt dieser Prozess zu neuen Arten.

Die zweite große Gruppe wird als Nicht-Mbunas bezeichnet. Diese Gruppe wurde bis 1989 als „Haplochromis" angesprochen, obwohl bereits seinerzeit auch andere Gattungen (z. B. *Aulonocara, Aristochromis*) zu dieser Gruppe gehörten. Die Malawisee-„Haplochromis" wurden 1989 von Eccles Lind Trewavas taxonomisch bearbeitet, wobei eine Vielzahl neuer Gattungen aufgestellt wurde. Der Ausdruck „Haplochromis" entfiel dadurch, so dass heute der Begriff „Nicht-Mbunas" verwendet wird. Gegenwärtig sind es 38 Gattungen, die die Gruppe der Nicht-Mbunas bilden.

Die Nicht-Mbunas sind generell nicht so stark felsorientiert und bewohnen fast jeden Lebensraum des Malawisees, darunter auch die weiten sandigen Zonen und das lichtarme Tiefwasser. Die Gesamtlängen der Nicht-Mbunas betragen etwa 10 bis 40 cm. Die meisten Arten werden aber nur ca. 15 cm groß. Entsprechend der weiten Verbreitung in verschiedensten Biotopen haben die Nicht-Mbunas fast jede Nahrungsquelle erschlossen. Angefangen von relativ unspezialisierten Alles- bzw. Kleintierfressern *(Protomelas, Mylochromis, Otopharynx)* lassen sich Planktonspezialisten *(Copadichromis)*, Raubfische *(Stigmatochromis, Rhamphochromis)* sowie Extremformen wie z. B. Flossen- und Schuppenfresser *(Corematodus, Docimodus)* und natürlich zahlreiche Übergangsformen bezüglich der Ernährung nachweisen. Bemerkenswert ist auch, dass manche Arten ein geradezu skuriles Beutesuchverhalten entwickelt haben. *Mylochromis labidodon* dreht kleine Steine um und erbeutet die unter Steinen lebenden Kleintiere. *Protomelas fenestratus* bläst einen Wasserstrahl in das Sediment, um seine Beute freizulegen.

Analog zu den Mbunas, leben alle Arten endemisch im Malawisee. Eine weitere Gemeinsamkeit besteht darin, dass alle Arten der beiden Gruppen Maulbrüter im weiblichen Geschlecht sind.

Abschließend ist anzumerken, dass es im Malawisee neben den Mbunas und Nicht-Mbunas eine Handvoll weiterer Buntbarsche gibt. Hierzu zählen *Tilapia rendalli*, der einzige substratbrütende Cichlide des Sees, *Astatotilapia calliptera*, *Serranochromis robustus* sowie einige *Oreochromis*-Arten. Die genannten Arten lassen sich nicht den Mbunas oder Nicht-Mbunas zurechnen, sondern weisen enge verwandtschaftliche Beziehungen zu flussbewohnenden Buntbarschen aus der Umgebung des Malawisees auf.

Lebensräume des Malawisees

Es ist völlig offensichtlich, dass in einem so riesigen Gewässer, wie es der Malawisee darstellt, eine Vielzahl von unterschiedlichsten Lebensräumen existiert. Der menschliche Hang zur Klassifizierung mag hier deshalb gekünstelt anmuten, gleichwohl dient die nachfolgende Einteilung in sieben Lebensraum-Typen, die bereits zu Beginn der 1960er veröffentlicht wurde, der besseren Übersicht. Dem Aquarianer erleichtert die Kenntnis der einzelnen Lebensräume die naturnahe Einrichtung des Aquariums.

Wenn man aquaristische Reiseberichte vom Malawisee liest, so kann man den Eindruck gewinnen, die meisten Küsten dieses Sees bestünden aus steilen Felsufern. Zwar stammen die meisten Aquarienfische von felsigen Uferbereichen, doch der überwiegende Teil (ca. 70 %) der Küstenlinien wird von flach abfallenden Sandzonen gebildet. Mbunas wird man hier kaum antreffen, wohl aber verschiedene „Sandcichliden" aus der Gruppe der Nicht-Mbunas. Insbesondere die *Lethrinops*-Artigen *(Lethrinops, Taeniolethrinops* und *Tramitichromis)* sowie auch zahlreiche *Nyassachromis* treten über Sandgrund in großer Anzahl auf. An manchen Stellen lassen sich sogenannte Laichkolonien beobachten, in denen sich Hunderte von Männchen, die um die Gunst der Weibchen werben, dicht an dicht mit ihren Revieren bzw. Laichburgen befinden. Tendenziell sind die meisten Sandbewohner weniger plakativ gefärbt als die Bewohner der Fels- und Übergangszonen.

Im optischen wie auch hinsichtlich der Artenzahl krassen Gegensatz stehen die **Felsküsten**, die die Haupt-Lebensräume der meisten für die Aquaristik gefangenen Arten darstellen. Gleichwohl, betrachtet man das flächenbezogene Ausmaß felsiger oder steiniger Bereiche im Malawisee, so nimmt dieser Lebensraum weniger als 5 % der potentiell besiedelbaren Flächen ein. Fast alle Mbunas werden in den Felsbezirken angetroffen. Verschiedene Gattungen der Nicht-Mbunas sind gleichfalls hier verbreitet. Der Felsaufwuchs stellt für die meisten Cichliden die Nahrungsgrundlage dar.

Einen mitunter nur schwer abgrenzbaren Lebensraum stellt die sogenannte **Übergangszone** dar (engl. intermediate zone). An vielen Stellen laufen Sand- und Steinbereiche ineinander über. Sowohl Felsaufwuchs als auch freiliegende Sedimentflächen mit bodenbewohnenden Kleintieren stehen zur Nahrungssuche zur Verfügung. Derartige Bereiche zählen zu den artenreichsten Biotopen, da sie als „Nahtstellen" der Sand- und Felszonen entsprechend vielen Arten einen geeigneten Lebensraum bieten. Eine miniaturisierte Übergangszone lässt sich leider nur in sehr großflächigen Aquarien nachgestalten, da sich die Malawisee-Cichliden, wenn sie sich erst einmal im Aquarium eingelebt haben, nicht so sehr an bestimmte Bereiche gebunden fühlen und dann alle Zonen im Aquarium wahllos besiedeln. Der nächste Stein als Rückzugsmöglichkeit ist ja nicht weit entfernt, so dass sich ein Mbuna ohne Hemmungen in die kleine Aquariensandzone wagen kann, um ein *Nyassachromis*-Männchen mal kurz von seinem Sandkrater zu verscheuchen.

Die verbleibenden vier Lebensräume sind für den Aquarianer nur von untergeordnetem Interesse. Beim Freiwasser ist zu unterscheiden zwischen dem **ufernahen Freiwasser** und dem eigentlichen Pelagial, dem **uferfernen Freiwasser**. Letzteres wird strikt genommen nur von einer einzigen Art im Malawisee bewohnt, welche nicht zu den Cichliden, sondern zu den Sardellen zählt *(Engraulicypris sardella*, die Malawisee-Sardelle). Die sogenannten Utaka *(Copadichromis)* sind zwar Freiwasserbewohner, doch halten sich die Arten dieser Gattung stets im ufernahen Freiwasser auf. Die Nachahmung eines ufernahen Freiwassers für die Haltung von *Copadichromis*-Arten im Aquarium wäre simpel, wenn nicht die Dimensionen des betreffenden Lebensraums so gewaltig wären. Ein möglichst großes (hohes wie tiefes) Aquarium mit viel freiem Schwimmraum sowie einer felsigen Rückwand wäre ausreichend. Allerdings, die meisten der für die Aquaristik eingeführten *Copadichromis* lassen sich in den üblichen Aquarien problemlos dauerhaft pflegen und züchten.

Einen ganz besonderen Lebensraum bildet die **Tiefwasserzone**. Hierunter versteht man üblicherweise den Tiefenbereich, deutlich unterhalb von etwa 30 Metern Tiefe, der im Malawisee bis etwa 200-250 Meter reicht. Noch tiefer ist das Wasser mit giftigem Schwefelwasserstoff angereichert, so dass kein höheres Leben mehr bestehen kann. In der Tiefwasserzone leben vorzugsweise Vertreter der Gattungen *Diplotaxodon, Alticorpus, Pallidochromis* sowie manche große *Rhamphochromis*-Arten. *Alticorpus*-Arten sind übrigens noch in fast 160 Metern Tiefe gefangen worden. Für aquaristische Belange sind alle typischen Tiefwasserbewohner ohne Bedeutung.

Den letzten Lebensraum, der hier vorgestellt werden soll, bilden **Flussmündungen** sowie mit Röhricht und **Schilf bestandene Ufer**. In diesen Bereichen finden sich meist Arten, die auch in den Flüssen leben, die in den Malawisee münden, aber durchaus auch Vertreter der Nicht-Mbunas. Von den Zierfisch-Exporteuren werden diese Uferabschnitte in der Regel gemieden, da sie meist unergiebig sind.

Pflege und Zucht

Die meisten Malawisee-Cichliden sind robuste und anpassungsfähige Pfleglinge. Es gilt nur wenige grundsätzliche Faktoren zu beachten, um diese schönen Buntbarsche dauerhaft zu halten und auch züchten zu können.

Das Wasser des Malawisees ist alkalisch, d. h., der pH-Wert liegt oberhalb des Neutralpunktes von 7,0. Meist werden pH-Werte von 7,5 bis 8,8 gemessen. Manche Aquarianer sind der Ansicht, dass man Malawisee-Cichliden am besten in hartem Wasser pflegen sollte. Dies trifft so nicht zu. Im Malawisee liegt die Gesamthärte bei 4-6 °dGH, so dass das Wasser als weich einzustufen ist. Die Karbonathärte liegt bei etwa 6-8 °. Wahr ist aber, dass hartes Wasser oft einen alkalischen pH-Wert aufweist, wodurch sich die o. g. Einschätzung erklärt. In den meisten Leitungswässern lassen sich Malawisee-Cichliden gut pflegen. Eine hohe Gesamthärte ist im üblichen Rahmen dem Wohlbefinden der Tiere übrigens nicht abträglich. Liegt der pH-Wert unterhalb des Neutralpunktes, sollte eine entsprechende Korrektur erfolgen (im Handel sind entsprechende Aufbereitungspräparate erhältlich). Die Wassertemperatur sollte, entsprechend den Verhältnissen im See, zwischen 24-26 °C liegen.

Bei der Beckeneinrichtung ist als Bodengrund grober, nicht zu heller Sand zu empfehlen. Feiner Sand hat den Nachteil, dass beim Scheibenreinigen leicht Sandpartikel in den Schwamm gelangen, die dann die Scheibe verkratzen. Kies mit einer Körnung von 3-5 mm, wie er insbesondere in den 70er und 80er Jahren in der Aquaristik verwendet wurde, ist nicht so gut geeignet, da einerseits kleinere Arten den Untergrund nicht mehr nach Nahrung durchsuchen können, andererseits wird das Anlegen von Laichgruben und -kratern erschwert.

Bei der Inneneinrichtung kommen grundsätzlich alle Materialien in Betracht, die sich nicht nachteilig auf die Wasserqualität auswirken und den ästhetischen Anforderungen des Pflegers gerecht werden. Üblicherweise werden verschiedene Sorten von Steinen verwandt, mit denen man Versteckmöglichkeiten für unterlegene Exemplare und tragende Weibchen schaffen sollte. Damit sich die revierverteidigenden Männchen nicht immer gleich sehen, empfiehlt es sich, das Becken mit Aufbauten oder Sichtblenden zu gliedern.

Pflanzen spielen im natürlichen Lebensraum keine wesentliche Rolle. Im Aquarium kann man robuste Pflanzen aber ohne weiteres einsetzen. Bewährt haben sich Riesenvallisnerien, *Cryptocorynen (C. usteriana)*, Javafarn sowie *Anubias*. Die beiden letztgenannten Arten wurzeln frei auf Steinen und anderen rauhen Gegenständen, so dass sie sich besonders zur Begrünung einer Felsrückwand anbieten.

Eine allgemein verbindliche Regel für die Einrichtung eines Malawisee-Cichliden-Aquariums gibt es (Gott sei Dank) nicht. Hier kann jeder mit mehr oder weniger Steinaufbauten und/oder Pflanzen zum gewünschten Erfolg kommen.

Von großer Bedeutung ist die Fütterung. Die meisten Aquarianer machen den Fehler, dass sie zu viel und mit zu „schwerer" Kost füttern. Vor allem Mbunas sind als Aufwuchsfresser „leichte", d. h. ballastreiche Kost gewöhnt (Wildfänge naturgemäß mehr als Nachzuchten). Schieres Fleisch (z. B. Rinderherz, Fisch) sollte deshalb gar nicht oder nur selten in geringen Mengen an Mbunas verfüttert werden. Es ist vorteilhaft, Mbunas des öfteren mit Grünflocken *(Spirulina)* oder anderer pflanzlicher Kost zu füttern. Ansonsten bieten sich die üblichen Flocken- und Frostfuttersorten zur Ernährung an (adulte *Artemia*, Rote Mückenlarven, *Mysis*, Wasserflöhe, *Cyclops*).

Wesentlich unempfindlicher verhalten sich da die Nicht-Mbunas. Sie können schon mal einen deftigen Brocken vertragen, insbesondere die größeren räuberischen Arten. Mit den oben genannten Futtermitteln lassen sich sonst die meisten der Nicht-Mbunas zufriedenstellend ernähren. Bei den Futtermengen braucht man allerdings nicht so vorsichtig wie bei den Mbunas zu sein.

Allein die unterschiedlichen Nahrungsansprüche sprechen dafür, dass man Mbunas und Nicht-Mbunas nicht in einem Becken pflegen sollte. Trotzdem ist eine Vergesellschaftung beider Gruppen in vielen Fällen aquaristische Praxis. Man kann sich behelfen, indem man z. B. den größeren Nicht-Mbunas gezielt größere Brocken mit der Hand verabreicht, während die Mbunas mit pflanzlichem Flockenfutter auskommen müssen.

Unabhängig von den gruppen- und artspezifischen Unterschieden ist zu betonen, dass Malawisee-Cichliden einen großen Stoffumsatz haben. Eine kräftige Filterung und, wichtiger, ein regelmäßiger Teilwasserwechsel von etwa 30-40 % des Beckeninhaltes in Abständen von etwa 2-3 Wochen sind deshalb eine unabdingbare Voraussetzung.

Ein ganz bedeutender Faktor bei der Pflege ist die Beckengröße. Je größer das Becken, desto geringer die Probleme bei der Vergesellschaftung der verschiedenen Arten. Wer in einem 200-l-Becken eine Gemeinschaft verschiedener Arten pflegt, muss sich darauf einrichten, des öfteren regulierend einzugreifen. Das heißt, unterlegene Tiere oder mitunter auch ein aggressives Männchen müssen aus dem Becken entfernt werden, um den „Frieden" zu wahren. Ab einer Größe von etwa 600 l nimmt die Notwendigkeit des „Regulierens" bis auf ein Minimum ab. Beckengrößen über 1000 l lassen ernsthafte Aggressionen kaum aufkommen bzw. Aggressionen „verpuffen" wirkungslos, weil die attackierten und unterlegenen Exemplare problemlos ausweichen können. Natürlich spielt bei der obigen Betrachtung auch die Größe und das Aggressionspotential der gepflegten Arten eine entscheidende Rolle. In 30 cm großes *Dimidochromis-kiwinge*-Männchen ist leicht in der Lage, die gesamte Belegschaft eines 1000-l-Aquariums in Schach zu halten. Die Ausführungen beziehen sich deshalb nur auf üblicherweise in solchen Becken gepflegte Arten mit Gesamtlängen von etwa 12 bis 15 cm, in Einzelfällen bis 20 cm.

Ansonsten gelten bei der Vergesellschaftung von Malawisee-Cichliden die üblichen Regeln. Es ist selbstverständlich, dass man besonders aggressive Arten nicht mit durchsetzungsschwachen Cichliden zusammen pflegen sollte. Raubfische und große Malawisee-Cichliden sollten ebenfalls unter sich bleiben, genauso wie die sandbewohnenden *Nyassachromis*-Arten, wenn man sich an deren typischen Verhaltensweisen erfreuen möchte. Auch bei der Vergesellschaftung verschiedener Arten gilt, dass man umso unterschiedlichere Arten zusammen pflegen kann, je größer das Becken ist.

Oftmals wird die Frage nach der Zahl der Fische gestellt, die man sinnvollerweise pflegen sollte. Hierbei ist es wichtig zu wissen, dass die Auswirkungen von Aggressionen umso größer sind, je weniger Fische im Aquarium sind, weil sich die Aggressionen ja auf nur wenige Individuen verteilen, die vom Aggressor zudem noch gezielt attackiert werden. Dies ist in einem überbesetzten Aquarium viel weniger der Fall. Mehr noch: Ab einer bestimmten Besatzdichte nimmt das Revierverhalten der Männchen vollständig ab, einfach weil es nicht mehr möglich ist, ein Revier zu verteidigen. Auf diese Weise werden Aggressionen zwar vollständig unterbunden, doch lastet in einem solchen Becken wegen des Überbesatzes ein sehr hoher Stress auf den einzelnen Fischen, was zu Krankheiten und auch zeitweiliger Unfruchtbarkeit führen kann. Ein goldener Mittelweg ist also, wie so oft, zu empfehlen. Bei Mbunas hat sich z.B. ein Besatz von etwa 30 bis 40 ca. 7-10 cm großen Exemplaren in einem 2-Meter-Becken als guter Kompromiss erwiesen. Letztlich liegt es im Gespür des Pflegers, die Bestandsdichte unter seinen spezifischen Verhältnissen sinnvoll auszuwählen. Ein Patentrezept gibt es jedenfalls nicht.

Neben der Gesamtmenge der Fische im jeweiligen Aquarium stellt sich auch die Frage nach der Zahl der Cichliden ein und derselben Art. Üblicherweise wird empfohlen, ein Männchen mit mehreren Weibchen zu vergesellschaften. Allerdings, bei Arten, bei denen sich auch die Weibchen untereinander aggressiv verhalten, kann es mitunter unmöglich sein, zwei oder mehr Weibchen zu halten. Grundsätzlich kann festgestellt werden, dass es manchmal sehr schwierig ist, zwei Weibchen einer Art zu pflegen. Dagegen ist es bei den meisten Arten ohne weiteres möglich, fünf oder mehr Weibchen in einem Becken zu halten. Ganz wenige oder ganz viele, das scheint das beste Prinzip für besonders aggressive Arten zu sein. Was für die Weibchen gilt, trifft auch für die Zahl der Männchen zu, wobei zu berücksichtigen ist, dass die Pflege mehrerer Männchen nur in großen Becken sinnvoll ist (je nach Größe der betreffenden Art etwa ab +/-500 l). Eines ist bei der Pflege mehrerer Männchen ein großer Vorteil: Dadurch, dass ständig Nebenbuhler gegenwärtig sind, befinden sich die Männchen permanent in Prachtfärbung, allzeit bereit zu imponieren und ihren Bereich zu verteidigen.

Alle Malawisee-Cichliden sind, wie erwähnt, Maulbrüter im weiblichen Geschlecht. Eine Paarbindung zwischen den Geschlechtspartnern besteht nicht im eigentlichen Sinne, sondern ist auf die Phase des gemeinsamen Ablaichens beschränkt (sog. agame Maulbrüter). Das Ablaichen vollzieht sich bei den meisten Arten (soweit bekannt) unter kreisenden Bewegungen. Sofort nach der Eiablage dreht sich das Weibchen und nimmt die Eier ins Maul auf. Die gelben, Eiattrappen ähnlichen Flecke in der Afterflosse der meisten Männchen könnten die Funktion haben, die Weibchen zu animieren, nach den Afterflossenflecken zu schnappen, um dabei dann das Sperma der Männchen aufzunehmen (Wicklersche Eiattrappen-Theorie). Somit würden die Eier erst im Maul des Muttertieres befruchtet.

Bei dem überwiegenden Teil der aquaristisch bekannten Arten beträgt die Brutzeit in Abhängigkeit von der Wassertemperatur etwa 3 Wochen. Geringfügige Abweichungen nach oben und nach unten sind artabhängig möglich. Die entlassenen Jungtiere sind meist um 10 mm groß und bereits fertig entwickelt. Da die Jungtiere sofort Artemia-Nauplien und fein zerriebenes Flockenfutter annehmen, ist die Aufzucht in der Regel völlig problemlos.

Bei den Nicht-Mbunas werden die Jungtiere noch einige Tage noch dem ersten Entlassen bei vermeintlicher Gefahr und am Abend wieder ins Maul aufgenommen. Bei den Mbunas ist das Brutpflegeverhalten nach dem Freisetzen der Jungtiere deutlich schwächer ausgeprägt. Nach Aquarienbeobachtungen setzen viele Arten ihre Jungtiere frei und kümmern sich dann nicht mehr um sie.

Insgesamt betrachtet ist die Nachzucht von Malawisee-Cichliden denkbar einfach. Unter entsprechenden Bedingungen wird man es kaum vermeiden können, dass sich der Fortpflanzungstrieb seinen Weg bahnt. Wer die Jungtiere aufziehen möchte, sollte das Weibchen 1 bis 2 Wochen nach dem Ablaichen in ein separates Becken überführen.

The Lake

Lake Malawi, previously known as Lake Nyasa, lies in the southern section of the East African Rift valley. The north-south axis is almost 600 km long and the lake has a maximum breadth of ca. 80 km. Its surface area has been given as nearly 31000 km^2. The maximum depth is more than 700 m. This means that after Lake Victoria and Lake Tanganyika, Lake Malawi is the third largest lake in Africa.

This inland sea is bounded by three countries. Most of the coastline belongs to Malawi, which extends along almost the whole of the west coast and includes the southern coast up to the middle of the eastern shore; roughly 800 km in all. Mozambique borders on ca. 200 km of the central eastern coast. The north-eastern coast and a negligible part of the north-western coast belong to Tanzania forming a further 300 km of coastline. In Tanzania and in Mozambique this lake is still called Lake Nyasa, which in the language of the Yao means "great water".

Lake Malawi is really an unique body of water. When one takes a bath in the waves on one of the often extensive beaches, it is surprising to find that the water is not salty. In addition to the long flat sandy beaches there are stony and rocky coastal regions, in which especially the cichlids known as "Mbunas" are to be found. Wide river mouths and marshy shores covered with reeds complete the diverse landscape of Lake Malawi. A most prominent feature is the gigantic chains of mountains that frame the lake both on its north-west coast (north of Nkhata Bay) and its north-east coast (the Livingstone Mountains). These geographical formations illustrate impressively the structure of the rift valley through which Lake Malawi was formed approximately 1-2 million years ago.

There is no doubt that Lake Malawi's most special feature is its cichlids. More than 600 species are now known, though many of these still have to be described scientifically and are classified under working names or trade names (see below). Apart from a few exceptions, all these cichlids are endemic to Lake Malawi, which means that they are only found in this body of water and no where else in the world.

The Cichlids of Lake Malawi

Basically, die Lake Malawi cichlids can be divided into two large groups: the Mbunas and Non-Mbunas. Mbunas is the indigenous name for the cichlids living in the rocky littoral. Under this name is to be understood an almost self-contained (i.e. it is well differentiable from the other cichlids groups) group of small to medium-sized cichlids, which with only a few exceptions live in intimate association with the rocks. The basis of the Mbunas' diet is the rock aufwuchs which is grazed using a number of techniques – scraping, plucking or by combing through the algal carpet. It should be taken into account that the rock aufwuchs, or in general any aufwuchs which settles on hard substrates, although being mainly composed of algae and bacteria, it also includes a number of small organisms (e. g. insect larvae, crustaceans, small worms and snails). It is obvious that the aufwuchs grows especially well where there is a lot of solar energy available — i.e. in shallow water down to a depth of ca. 5 m. This is most probably the main reason why the majority of the Mbunas occur in shallow water. In extremely shallow waters (> ca. 1 m), only the strongest or most assertive species are found as they force their rivals into the deeper and therefore nutritionally poorer regions. Even though many species have developed special techniques for feeding on the aufwuchs, other sources of food are not rejected, especially if these are more easily available. If there is an abundance of plankton, the Mbunas can be seen in large groups feeding in open water. For many species, plankton forms the main part of the diet.

At this moment in time, the Mbunas have been classified in 12 genera: *Cyathochromis, Cynotilapia, Genyochromis, Gephyrochromis, Iodotropheus, Labeotropheus, Labidochromis, Maylandia, Melanochromis, Petrotilapia, Pseudotropheus* and *Tropheops*. A total of nearly 300 species are known. It is not possible to exactly say how many species there are as with some populations it has not as yet been definitely decided whether they are geographical forms of a known species or whether they actually are true species themselves. The smallest Mbunas grow only to a length of 6-7 cm (total length). The largest Mbunas are representatives of the genus Petrotilapia, whose males can even attain a length of 18 cm. The majority of the Mbunas have a length of 9-11 cm.

The close association of the Mbunas to the rocky substrate results in that the majority of the species are very sedentary. Furthermore, it is of significance that even small, only 20 m wide stretches of sand will not be crossed by many Mbunas. Due to this factor there are many isolated populations in existence which with time have undergone different developments and have, for example, formed different geovariants. Such processes will lead finally to the formation of new species.

The second large group of cichlids is known as the Non-Mbunas. Up until 1989, this group was referred to as "*Haplochromis*" even though at that time other genera (e.g. *Aulonocara, Aristochromis*) belonged to this group. The Lake Malawi "*Haplochromis*" were investigated taxonomically by Eccles and Trewavas in 1989. These scientists then set up a number of new genera. The term „Haplochromis" was rejected in favour of the term "Non-Mbunas". Nowadays, 38 genera are included in the group of the Non-Mbunas.

The Non-Mbunas are generaliy not so strongly rockorientated and live in almost every habitat available in Lake Malawi, including the wide sandy zones and the poorly lit depths. The total length of the Non-Mbunas varies from between 10 to 40 cm. The majority of these species are only ca. 15 cm long. In conjunction with their wide distribution in the various biotopes, the Non-Mbunas have taken over almost every food source. The Non-Mbunas include the relatively non-specialised omnivores or feeders on small organisms (*Protomelas, Mylochromis, Otopharynx*), plankton specialists (*Copadichromis*), predators (*Stigmatochromis, Rhamphochromis*) and extreme specialists such as fin or scale feeders (*Corematodus, Docimodus*) and naturally numerous transitional forms with respect to their nutritional requirements.

Finally, it should be noted that along with Mbunas and Non-Mbunas, there are a few other cichlids that live in Lake Malawi. These include *Tilapia rendalli*, the only substrate brooding cichlid found in the lake, *Astatotilapia calliptera*, *Serranochromis robustus* and a few *Oreochromiss* spp.. These species cannot be included in either the Mbunas or Non-Mbunas as they exhibit close relationships to the river-living cichlids from the region around Lake Malawi.

The Habitats Present In Lake Malawi

It is obvious that in a giant body of water like Lake Malawi there are a number of different habitats present. The human tendency for classification may appear often artificial, nevertheless the following division into seven habitats initially published at the beginning of the 1960s, provides the best overview. The knowledge of the individual habitats enables the aquarist to set up his aquarium as naturally as possible.

If one reads the aquaristic travel reports about Lake Malawi one gains the impression that the coast of this lake is mainly made up of cliffs. In contrast, although the majority of ornamental fish come from the rocky regions of the coast, most of the coastline (ca. 70 %) is formed by gradually inclining sandy zones. While Mbunas are only rarely found in these regions, the various "sand cichlids" from the group of the Non-Mbunas are at home here. Especially the *Lethrinops* spp. (*Lethrinops, Taeniolethrinops* and *Tramitichromis*), and the numerous *Nyassachromis* occur in large numbers over the sandy bottom. At some places so-called spawning colonies can be seen in which hundreds of males are found living side by side in their territories or sand nests, all trying to court the attention of the females. Most of the sand dwellers are not so colourful as the species found in the rocky or intermediate zones.

The rocky coast is not only crassly different optically but also the number of species living here varies greatly from the aforementioned sandy zone. This is the main habitat of the majority of the species caught for the ornamental fish trade. Nevertheless when one takes into consideration the total area covered by rocky or stony regions in Lake Malawi, this habitat only takes into account less than 5 % of the potential area available for the fish to settle. Despite this, virtually all the Mbunas are to be found in the rocky regions. Various Non-Mbuna genera are also to be found in these zones. The aufwuchs growing on the rocks is the main source of nutrients for the majority of these cichlids.

The intermediate zone is a habitat that can only be poorly demarcated. At many places the sand and stone regions run into each other. Here both aufwuchs and free-lying sediment with ground-living organisms are available as food sources. These areas belong to the most species-rich biotopes as their position as "junctions" between the sand and rock zones offer a suitable habitat to a large number of species. A miniature intermediate zone can only be built in a very large aquarium as the Lake Malawi cichlids when they have first begun to feel secure in an aquarium do not feel themselves bound to one particular area and settle higgledypiggledy throughout the zones present in the tank. The next sheltering stone is indeed not so far away, so that a Mbuna, without experiencing any reservations will be able to venture into the adjacent area of sand in order to quickly scare off a *Nyassachromis* male from his sand nest.

The remaining four habitats are only of minor importance to the aquarist. Open water should be differentiated in the open water close to the shore and the pelagic environment (the open water far away from the shore). Strictly speaking the latter zone is only inhabited by a single species which does not belong to the cichlids but to the anchovies (*Engraulicypris sardella*, the Lake Malawi anchovy). The so-called Utaka (*Copadichromis*) are indeed inhabitants of open water but these species always remain in the open water close to the shore. The reproduction of this habitat in captivity for the keeping of the *Copadichromis* spp. would be simple if its dimensions were not so huge. The largest possible aquarium (both in height and floor area) with lots of swimming room and a rocky back wall would be sufficient. Despite this, the majority of the imported *Copadichromis* can be permanently maintained and bred in a standard aquarium.

A very special habitat is formed by the deep water zone. This is normally considered as the depths below 30 m and in Lake Malawi this extends down to 200-250 m. Further down in the lake, the water is contaminated by poisonous hydrogen sulphide making the survival of higher organisms impossible. In the deep water zones live chiefly representatives of the genera *Diplotaxodon, Alticorpus, Pallidochromis* and some large *Rhamphochromis* spp. Especially the tasty *Rhamphochromis* and *Diplotaxodon* spp. are often caught by fishermen, so that these deep water inhabitants now and again are seen on the lake. *Alticorpus* spp. have been caught at depths of almost 160 m. None of the typical deep water dwellers are of interest for the aquaristic.

The final habitat which will be introduced here is formed by the river mouths and the reed-covered shore line. In these regions there can be found not only those species which also live in the rivers that flow into Lake Malawi (*Tilapia, Astatotilapia, Serranochromis*), but also representatives of the Non-Mbunas. The exporters of ornamental fish tend to shun these areas as they are usually unproductive.

Husbandry and Breeding

The majority of Lake Malawi cichlids are robust and adaptable pets. Only a few basic factors must be considered in order to be able to permanently keep these beautiful cichlids and to breed them.

The water of Lake Malawi is alkaline, meaning that the pH lies above the neutral point of 7.0. Mainly pH values of between 7.5 to 8.8 have been measured. Some aquarists are of the opinion that one can keep Lake Malawi cichlids best of all in hard water — this is not true. In Lake Maiawi, the total water hardness is between 4-6 °dGH, so that the water is definitely soft. The carbonate hardness lies between 68 °. It is certainly true that hard water often has an alkaline pH, which explains the erroneous assumption. Lake Malawi cichlids can be kept well in most supplies of tap water. A high total hardness in the usual range found in normal tap water is not detrimental to the health of the fish. If the pH lies below the neutral point then it should be corrected (suitable preparations are commercially available). The water temperature should be between 24-26 °C in order to mimic the conditions in the lake.

A coarse sand that is not too light in colour is to be recommended for the decoration of the tank. Fine sand has the disadvantage that during the cleaning of the glass panes, the grains are easily taken up by the sponge and scratch the glass. Gravel with a grain size of 3-5 mm, as preferred in the 1970s and the 1980s is not so suitable as on the one hand, the smaller species are not able to search through the bottom for food and on the other hand the building of spawning hollows and sand nests is made niore difficult.

Basically all those materials which do not have an adverse effect on the water quality and fit the aesthetic sensitivities of the keeper can be used for the interior decoration of the tank. Normally, different types of stones are used to form hiding places for subdominant individuals and brooding females. So that the territorial males do not have to always see each other, it is recommended to place sight barriers and other constructions in the tank.

Plants do not play an important role in the natural habitat of these fish. In the aquarium robust plants can be planted without any problems. The giant vallisneria, *Cryptocorynia* (*C. usteriana*), Java fern and *Anubias* have proven to be suitable. The latter two species root on stones or other rough surfaces and are therefore suitable for planting on a rocky back wall. A general compulsory rule for the setting up of a Lake Malawi cichlid aquarium is (thankfully) not available. Everyone can achieve the desired success with a greater or smaller number of rock formations and/or plants.

Of great importance is the diet fed to these cichlids. The majority of aquarists make the mistake that they give too much and too "heavy" a diet. Especially the aufwuchs-feeding Mbunas are used to a "light" or roughage-rich diet (fish from the wild naturally more than captive-bred fish). Pure meat (e.g. beef heart, fish) should therefore never be given to Mbunas or only rarely in small amounts. It is advantageous to feed Mbunas often with green flakes (Spirulina) or other vegetable foods. Otherwise, the other flaked feeds or frozen foods (adult Artemia, red guat larvae, Mysis, Water fleas, Cyclops) may be given.

The Non-Mbunas are in comparison less sensitive. They can now and again cope with a large chunk of meat, especially the arger predatory species. With the aforementioned diet, the Non-Mbunas can also be adequately nourished. Also it is not so necessary to be so careful about the amount of food fed to these species.

Their different nutritional requirements alone indicate that Mbunas and Non-Mbunas should not be maintained together in the same tank. Despite this, the keeping of members of these two groups together is often practised. One can help the situation by feeding the larger Non-Mbunas individually with large chunks of meat while The Mbunas are made to live on the vegetarian flaked feed.

Independent of the group and species-specific differences, it must be emphasised that the Lake Malawi cichlids have a high metabolism. A strong filtration system and more importantly a regular water change of 30-40 % of the tank's total volume every 2-3 weeks is a necessary prerequisite.

A major factor in the husbandry of these fish is the size of the tank. The bigger the tank the fewer the problems associated with the cohabatation of various spedes. Whoever keeps a stock of various species in a 200-L-tank must be prepared to be often involved in regulatinig the fish population. This means that subdominant fish or an aggressive male must be removed from the tank in order to maintain the "peace". With tanks of about 600 L is this type of regulation reduced to a minimum. In tanks of 1000 L, aggression rarely develops or if it does, it fizzles out without any adverse effects as the attakking and subdominant individuals can easily evade each other. Naturally, this situation depends largely on the size and aggression potential of the species being kept. A 30-cm-long *Dimidiochromis kiwinge* male is quite capable of keeping the whole stock of a 1000-L aquarium in check. The aforementioned suggestions are in respect of the species usually kept in a standard aquarium and that have a total body length of 12 to 15 cm; in individual cases up to 20 cm. Otherwise the rules for the cohabitation of Lake Malawi cichlids are as normal. It is obvious that one should not keep the very aggressive species with the less assertive cichlids. Predators and the large Lake Malawi cichlids should also be maintained alone. This is also true for the sand-dwelling *Nyassachromis* spp., if one wishes to enjoy their typical behaviour patterns. In addition, with the cohabitation of various species, the rule is: the more diverse the species the larger the size of the tank required.

Often the question arises about the number of fish which can be sensibly maintained together. Here it is important to note that the lower the number of fish present in the aquarium the greater the effects of aggression. This is because the aggression can only be directed at a few individuals who are then attakked by the aggressor. This is rarely the case in a overpopulated aquarium. Addiditionally, at a certain population density the territorial behaviour of the males is totally diminished, simply because it is no longer possible to defend a territory. In this way aggression is totally undermined, but in such tanks the individual fish are subjected to a very high degree of stress which may lead to disease and temporary infertility. The golden mean is, as so often, to be recommended. With Mbunas, a population of 30 to 40 fish with a length of 7-10 cm in a 2-metre-tank has proved to be a good compromise. Finally, the skill of the keeper is required in deciding which population density is suitable for his conditions. There is no magic formula.

In conjunction with the total number of fish that can be held in a specific aquarium, the question arises about the suitable number of cichlids from a specific species. Normally it is recommended to keep one male with a number of females. However, in those species where the females are aggressive to each other it may be impossible to keep two or more females together. Basically it has been ascertained that it is sometimes very difficult to keep two females from the same species together. Only a very few or very many appears to be the best principle for especially aggressive species. What is applicable to the females also holds true for the males, whereby it must be taken into consideration that the keeping of a number of males together is only sensible in a large tank (depending on the size of the species: ±/-500 L). One thing is of great advantage in the maintenance of a number of males together – as there arc always rivals present, the males remain permanently in their most colourful "dress" so that they are constantly ready to display and to defend their territory.

All Lake Malawi cichlids as mentioned previously, are maternal mouthbrooders. The formation of breeding pairs between the sexes does not actually occur as they remain together only during spawning (so-called agamic mouthbrooders). Spawning occurs in the majority of the spedies (as known so far) during circling. Immediately after the female has laid her eggs she turns round and takes them into her mouth. The yellow eggspot-like blotches in the anal fin of the majority of the males may have the function of animating the females to snap at them so that they will take up the male's spermatozoa into their mouths (Wickler's Egg Dummy Theory). Subsequently, the eggs are fertilised in the mouth of the mother fish.

In the majority of the aquaristically known species the brooding period, depending on water temperature, takes about 3 weeks. Small variations are possible according to species differences. The fry are usually ca. 10 mm long when released and are fully developed. As the young fish are immediately capable of ingesting Artemia nauplii and finely crumbled flaked feed, rearing usually does not present any problems.

In the Non-Mbunas, during the next few days after their release, the fry are taken back into the mother's mouth in the advent of possible danger and in the evening. In the Mbunas the brooding behaviour after the release of the fry is distinctly weaker. According to observations in captivity many of these species release their fry and take no further notice of them.

All in all, the breeding of Lake Malawi cichlids is very easy. Under suitable conditions it is almost unadvoidable that the breeding instinct will take its own course. Whoever wishes to raise the young fish should place the females into a separate tank 1 to 2 weeks after spawning.

Namen

Es gibt zwei Arten von Namen: wissenschaftliche und nicht-wissenschaftliche. Während wissenschaftliche Namen grundsätzlich weltweit gültig und anerkannt sind, läßt sich dies bei den nicht-wissenschaftlichen Namen, den sogenannten Handels- oder Arbeitsnamen, wahrlich nicht behaupten. Wissenschaftliche Namen bestehen aus einem Gattungs- und Artnamen. Beide Namen werden *kursiv* geschrieben, der Artname wird stets klein geschrieben.

Buntbarsche (und natürlich auch andere Fische), die wissenschaftlich noch nicht beschrieben sind und somit noch keinen wissenschaftlichen Namen erhalten haben, werden üblicherweise mit vorläufigen Bezeichnungen belegt, bis eine wissenschaftliche Erstbeschreibung erfolgt. Meist ist es möglich, die Gattung zu bestimmen, in die eine neue Art einzuordnen ist, so dass nur ein Name zur Artbezeichnung geschaffen werden muss. Um kenntlich zu machen, daß es sich nicht um einen wissenschaftlichen Namen handelt, wird der Handels- oder Arbeitsname in Anführungszeichen gesetzt und nicht kursiv geschrieben. Um den Unterschied noch deutlicher zu machen, empfiehlt es sich, alle nicht-wissenschaftlichen Namen groß zu schreiben (z. B. *Pseudotropheus* „Red Top Ndumbi"). Manche Autoren setzen zwischen Gattungs- und Artnamen ein „spec." oder „sp." für species = Art, um hervorzuheben dass es sich um eine noch unbeschriebene Art handelt. Dies ist aus Sicht des Verfassers nicht notwendig und stört die alphabetische Einordnung. Aus diesem Grunde wird dieser Zusatz im Folgenden nicht verwendet. Die Anführungszeichen sowie die Großschreibweise sollten ausreichend sein, um zu verdeutlichen daß es sich um eine wissenschaftlich unbeschriebene Art handelt.

Der Zusatz „cf." (conferre = vergleiche) vor der Artbezeichnung bedeutet, dass es sich bei dem betreffenden Cichliden um die besagte Art handeln könnte (z. B. *Copadichrornis* cf. *tiavimanus*), aber keine ausreichende Sicherheit bei der Bestimmung des Fisches erlangt wurde. Wird dagegen der Zusatz „spec. aff." (species affinis = verwandte Art) verwendet, soll damit verdeutlicht werden, dass es sich nicht um die betreffende, aber eine eng verwandte Art handelt (z. B. *Pseudotropheus* spec. aff. *minutus*).

Einteilung der Arten

Entsprechend den beiden großen Cichlidengruppen im Malawisee wurde der Katalog zweigeteilt: Zuerst werden die Mbunas, danach die Nicht-Mbunas in alphabetischer Reihenfolge vorgestellt. Die wenigen Cichliden, die zu keiner der beiden Gruppen gehören, werden ganz am Ende des Katalogs aufgeführt (*Astatotilapia*, *Oreochromis*, *Serranochromis* und *Tilapia*).

Bildsymbole

Um einige wesentliche Informationen zu den abgebildeten Cichliden darzustellen, werden Bildsymbole verwandt, die weitgehend selbsterklärend sind. Es liegt in der Natur der Sache, daß einfache Bildsymbole keine differenzierten Angaben zulassen. Zur korrekten Einordnung der auf den Bildsymbolen enthaltenen Informationen ist es deshalb sinnvoll, die **Anmerkungen am Schluss dieses Bandes** zu berücksichtigen.

Hinsichtlich des Fortpflanzungsverhaltens wurde kein Bildsymbol verwendet, da bis auf eine Ausnahme alle Buntbarsche des Malawisees Maulbrüter im weiblichen Geschlecht sind (Ausnahme: *Tilapia rendalli*, Substratbrüter).

Names

There are two types ot names: scientific and non-scientific. While scientific names are in principle applicable and recognised throughout the world, this is not true of the non-scientific names (the so-called trade or working names). Scientific names include a genus and a species name. Both names are written in italics and the species name is always written starting wiih a small letter.

Cichlids (and naturally other fish) which have not been scientifically described and so have not been given a scientific name are given provisional names until the scientific first description has taken place. Usually it is possible to determine to which genus the new species belongs so that only a species name must be decided upon. In order to make it obvious that it is not a scientific name, the trade or working name will be written in quotation marks and not in italics. In order to make the difference even more pronounced, it is recommended that all the non-scientitic names should be written starting with a capital letter (e.g. *Pseudotropheus* "Red Top Ndumbi"). Some authors place a "spec." or "sp." (meaning species) in the name to underline that it is an undescribed species. This is in the opinion of the present author unnecessary and causes problems with the alphabetical categorisation of the species. Due to this reason, this abbreviation will not be used in the following. The quotation marks and the capitalisation are adequate for the indication that the specics has not been described scientifically.

The additional abbreviation "cf." (conferre = compare) before the species name indicates that the cichlid could be the named species (e.g. *Copadichromis* cf. *flavimanus*), but that there has not been sufficient certainty in the categorisation of the fish. If the abbreviation "spec. aff." (species affinis related species) is used, this means that it is not the stated species but a closely related one (e.g. *Pseudotropheus* spec. aff. *minutus*).

Arrangement of the Species

In conjunction with the fact that there are two large cichlid groups present in Lake Malawi (see above), the catalogue is divided into two: firstly the Mbunas and then the Non-Mbunas are introduced in alphabetical order. The small number of cichlids which do not belong to either of these two groups are presented at the back of the catalogue (*Astatotilapia*, *Oreochromis*, *Serranochromis* and *Tilapia*).

Picture Symbols

In order to present some important information about the depicted cichlids, pictographs are used which are mainly self-evident. Of course this type of simple pictorial representation does not allow for the presentation of greatly differentiated information. To acquire the correct classification of the information present within the pictographs, it is sensible to take note of the comments at the end of this catalogue. With respect to breeding behaviour no pictographs has been used as apart from one exception (*Tilapia rendalli*, substrate brooder), all the cichlids from Lake Malawi are maternal mouthbrooders.

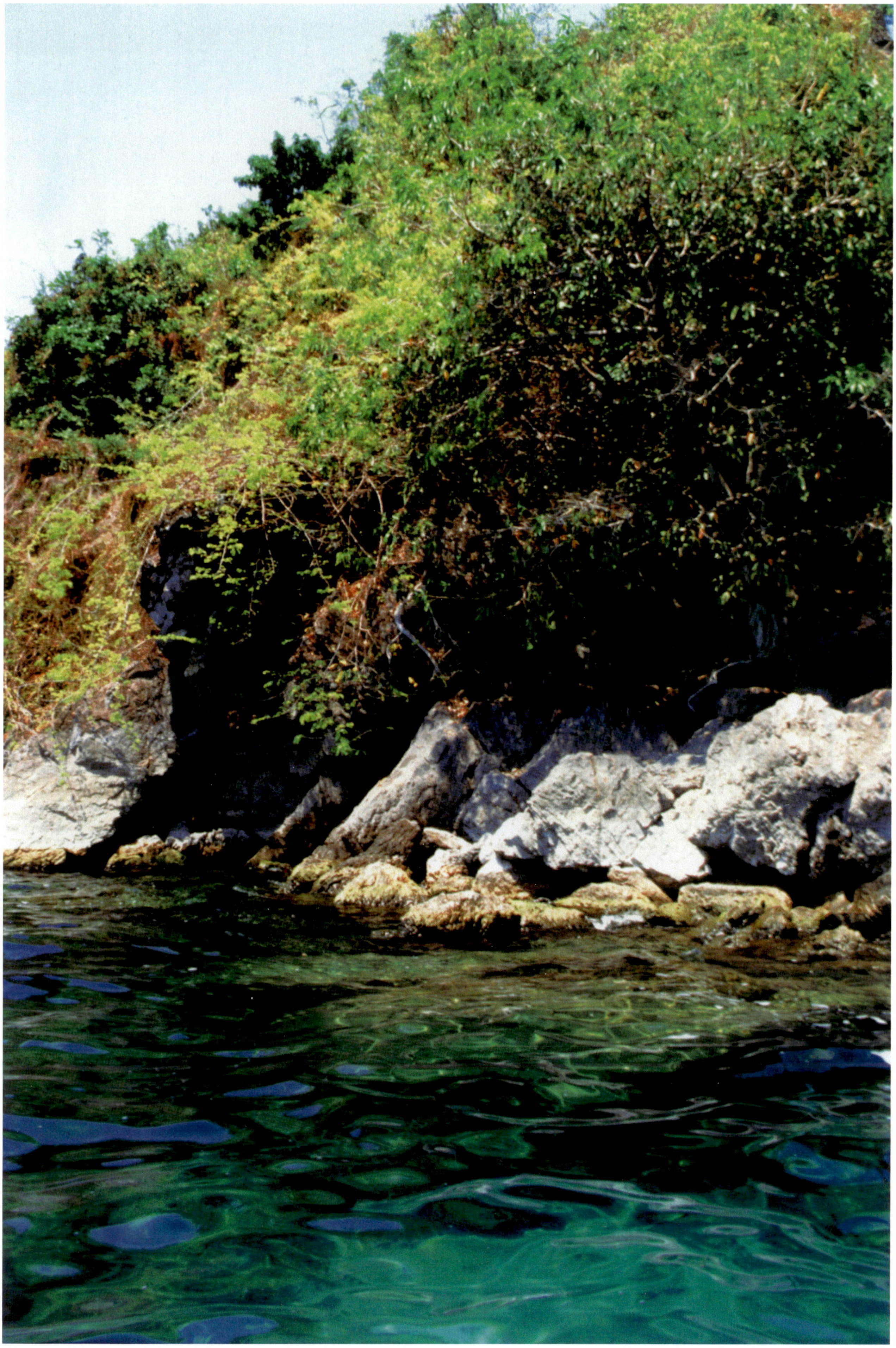

Cyathochromis obliquidens Trewavas, 1935

Khuyu/Likoma Island, Malawi

Cyathochromis obliquidens ♀ Trewavas, 1935

Madimba/Likoma Island, Malawi

Cynotilapia afra (Günther, 1893)

Aquarium

Cynotilapia afra ♀ (Günther, 1893)

Aquarium

Cynotilapia afra (Günther, 1893)

Nkhata Bay, Malawi

Cynotilapia afra (Günther, 1893)

Lions Cove, Malawi

Cynotilapia afra (Günther, 1893)

Magunga, Tanzania

Cynotilapia afra (Günther, 1893)

Ndumbi Reef, Tanzania

Cynotilapia afra (Günther, 1893)
Hongi Island, Tanzania

Cynotilapia afra (Günther, 1893)
Mbamba Bay/Mara Rocks, Tanzania

Cynotilapia afra (Günther, 1893)
Hai Reef, Tanzania

Cynotilapia afra (Günther, 1893)
Chilanje/Chisumulu Island, Malawi

Cynotilapia afra (Günther, 1893)
Mbuzi Island/Likoma Island, Malawi

Cynotilapia afra (Günther, 1893)
Ndumbi Rocks/Likoma Island, Malawi

Cynotilapia afra (Günther, 1893)
Kanjindo, Mozambique

Cynotilapia afra (Günther, 1893)
Mara Point/Cobue, Mozambique

Cynotilapia axelrodi Burgess, 1976
Aquarium Nkhata-Bay-Population, Malawi

Cynotilapia axelrodi Burgess, 1976
Nkhata Bay, Malawi

Cynotilapia "Black Dorsal"
Mbenji Island, Malawi

Cynotilapia "Black Eastern"
Makanjila, Malawi

Cynotilapia "Black Eastern"
Tumbi Point, Mozambique

Cynotilapia "Chinyankwazi"
Chinyankhwazi, Malawi

Cynotilapia "Jalo"
Aquarium

Cynotilapia "Jalo" ♀
Aquarium

Cynotilapia "Lion"

Aquarium Lions-Cove-Population

Cynotilapia "Lion"

Manda, Tanzania

Cynotilapia "Lion"

Lions Cove, Malawi

Cynotilapia "Lion"

Manda, Tanzania

Cynotilapia "Mbamba"

Chitendi Island, Malawi

Cynotilapia "Mbamba"

Nkhata Bay, Malawi

Cynotilapia "Mbamba"

Nkhata Bay, Malawi

Cynotilapia "Mbamba"

Chilanje/Chisumulu Island, Malawi

Cynotilapia "Ndumbi"

Ndumbi Rocks/Likoma Island, Malawi

Cynotilapia "Ndumbi"

Ndumbi Rocks/Likoma Island, Malawi

Cynotilapia "Thomasi"
(= Cynotilapia "Mbweca")

Mara Point/Cobue, Mozambique

Cynotilapia "Yellow Dorsal"

Mbenji Island, Malawi

Genyochromis mento Trewavas, 1935

Mumbo Island, Malawi

Genyochromis mento Trewavas, 1935

N´tekete/Makanjila, Malawi

Cynotilapia mento Trewavas, 1935

Mara Point/Cobue, Mozambique

Cynotilapia mento Trewavas, 1935

Chirwa Island/Chilumba

Gephyrochromis cf. lawsi Fryer, 1957

N´tekete/Makanjila, Malawi

Gephyrochromis cf. lawsi Fryer, 1957

Aquarium

Gephyrochromis cf. moorii Boulenger, 1901

Aquarium

Gephyrochromis cf. moorii ♀

Aquarium

Gephyrochromis "Yellow"

Mbamba Bay, Tanzania

Gephyrochromis "Zebroides"

Masinje, Malawi

Iodotropheus sprengerae Oliver & Loiselle, 1972

Aquarium   Boadzulu-Island-Population, Malawi

Iodotropheus sprengerae ♀ Oliver & Loiselle, 1972

Aquarium   Boadzulu-Island-Population, Malawi

Labeotropheus fuelleborni Ahl, 1927

Thumbi West Island, Malawi

Labeotropheus fuelleborni Ahl, 1927

Katari Island/Chilumba, Malawi

Labeotropheus fuelleborni Ahl, 1927

Pombo Rocks, Tanzania

Labeotropheus fuelleborni Ahl, 1927

N'nosi Reef/Miluluka, Mozambique

Labeotropheus fuelleborni ♀ Ahl, 1927

N'nosi Reef/Miluluka, Mozambique

Labeotropheus fuelleborni ♂ OB Ahl, 1927

Aquarium

Labeotropheus fuelleborni ♂ OB Ahl, 1927

Aquarium

Labeotropheus fuelleborni ♀ OB Ahl, 1927

Aquarium

Labeotropheus trewavasae ♀ OB   Fryer, 1956

Thumbi West Isand, Malawi

Labeotropheus trewavasae   Fryer, 1956

Thumbi West Island, Malawi

Labeotropheus trewavasae   Fryer, 1956

Ponta Messuli, Mozambique

Labeotropheus trewavasae   Fryer, 1956

Mumbo Island, Malawi

Labeotropheus trewavasae ♀ O   Fryer, 1956

Aquarium

Labeotropheus trewavasae   Fryer, 1956

Chilumba, Malawi

Labeotropheus trewavasae   Fryer, 1956

Aquarium

Labeotropheus trewavasae   Fryer, 1956

Aquarium

Labidochromis "Black Dorsal"

Aquarium	Lundo Island-Population, Tanzania

Labidochromis "Black Dorsal" ♀

Lundo Island, Tanzania

Labidochromis "Black Dorsal"

Chinula/Mbamba Bay, Tanzania

Labidochromis "Blue/White"

Tumbi Reef, Tanzania

Labidochromis "Blue/White" ♀

Magunga, Tanzania

Labidochromis "Blunt Nose"

Cove Mountain, Tanzania

Labidochromis caeruleus　　　Fryer, 1956

Aquarium	Nkhata-Bay-Population, Malawi

Labidochromis caeruleus ♀　　　Fryer, 1956

Aquarium	Nkhata-Bay-Population, Malawi

Labidochromis chisumulae ♀   Lewis, 1982

Chisumulu Island, Malawi

Labidochromis chisumulae   Lewis, 1982

Chisumulu Island, Malawi

Labidochromis chisumulae   Lewis, 1982

Aquarium   Chisumulu-Island-Population, Malawi

Labidochromis "Deep Body"

Pombo Rock, Tanzania

Labidochromis flavigulis   Lewis, 1982

Aquarium

Labidochromis flavigulis ♀   Lewis, 1982

Aquarium

Labidochromis freibergi   Johnson, 1974

Aquarium   Likoma-Island-Population, Malawi

Labidochromis freibergi ♀   Johnson, 1974

Aquarium   Likoma-Island-Population, Malawi

Labidochromis gigas ♀ Lewis, 1982

Maingano/Likoma Island, Malawi

Labidochromis gigas Lewis, 1982

Mbuzi Island/Likoma Island, Malawi

Labidochromis "Gigas Chilumba"

Chirwa Island/Chilumba, Malawi

Labidochromis "Gigas Ngkuyo"

Ngkuyo Island/Mbamba Bay, Tanzania

Labidochromis heterodon Lewis, 1982

Boadzulu Island, Malawi

Labidochromis "Hongi"

Hongi Island, Tanzania

Labidochromis "Hongi" ♀

Aquarium Hongi-Island-Population, Tanzania

Labidochromis "Hongi"

Undu Point, Tanzania

Labidochromis ianthinus Lewis, 1982

Mbenji Island, Malawi

Labidochromis "Likomae"

Membe Point/Likoma Island, Malawi

Labidochromis "Likomae" ♀

Membe Point/Likoma Island, Malawi

Labidochromis lividus Lewis, 1982

Ndomo Point/Likoma Island, Malawi

Labidochromis "Luhuchi"

Luhuchi Rocks/Mbamba Bay, Tanzania

Labidochromis maculicauda Lewis, 1982

Katari Island/Chilumba, Malawi

Labidochromis maculicauda Lewis, 1982

Lundo Island, Tanzania

Labidochromis maculicauda Lewis, 1982

Nkhata Bay, Malawi

Labidochromis mbenji Lewis, 1982

Mbenji Island, Malawi

Labidochromis mylodon Lewis, 1982

Mumbo Island, Malawi

Labidochromis pallidus Lewis, 1982

Aquarium Nakanthenga-Island-Population, Malawi

Labidochromis pallidus Lewis, 1982

Fotobecken Nakanthenga Island, Malawi

Labidochromis pallidus Lewis, 1982

Nakanthenga Island, Malawi

Labidochromis "Perlmutt"

Aquarium

Labidochromis "Perlmutt"

Higga Reef/Mbamba Bay, Tanzania

Labidochromis "Perlmutt" ♀

Higga Reef/Mbamba Bay, Tanzania

Labidochromis "Red Top Mbamba Bay"
(= "L. Kimpuma"), (= "L. Mbamba")
Aquarium

Labidochromis "Red Top Mbamba Bay" ♀
Aquarium

Labidochromis strigatus ♀   Lewis, 1982

Membe Island/Chisumulu Island, Malawi

Labidochromis strigatus   Lewis, 1982

Chiteko/Chisumulu Island, Malawi

Labidochromis textilis   Oliver, 1972

Holotypus

Labidochromis cf. textilis   Oliver, 1972

Nyamizimu/Meponda, Mozambique

Labidochromis cf. textilis ♀   Oliver, 1972

Chuanga/Metangula, Mozambique

Labidochromis cf. textilis   Oliver, 1972

Nyamizimu/Meponda, Mozambique

Labidochromis vellicans ♀ Trewavas, 1935

Aquarium

Labidochromis vellicans Trewavas, 1935

Aquarium

Labidochromis "Yellow"

Aquarium

Labidochromis "Yellow"

Aquarium

Labidochromis "Yellow" Trewavas, 1935

Aquarium

Labidochromis "Zebra Eastern"

Labidochromis "Zebra Eastern"

Ngulo/Chiloelo, Mozambique

Labidochromis zebroides Lewis, 1982

Mazimbwe Island/Likoma Island, Malawi

Maylandia callainos   (Stauffer & Hert, 1992)

Chitendi Island/Chilumba, Malawi

Maylandia callainos ♂ W   (Stauffer & Hert, 1992)

Chewere/Chilumba, Malawi

Maylandia callainos   (Stauffer & Hert, 1992)

Fotobecken   Nkhata Bay, Malawi

Maylandia callainos ♀ W   (Stauffer & Hert, 1992)

Fotobecken   Nkhata Bay, Malawi

Maylandia emmittos   Stauffer et al., 1997
(ex: *Pseudotropheus* "Zebra Mpanga")

Mpanga Rocks/Chilumba, Malawi

Maylandia emmittos   Stauffer et al., 1997
(ex: *Pseudotropheus* "Zebra Mpanga")

Mpanga Rocks/Chilumba, Malawi

Maylandia estherae   (Konings, 1995)

Aquarium

Maylandia estherae ♀   (Konings, 1995)

Aquarium

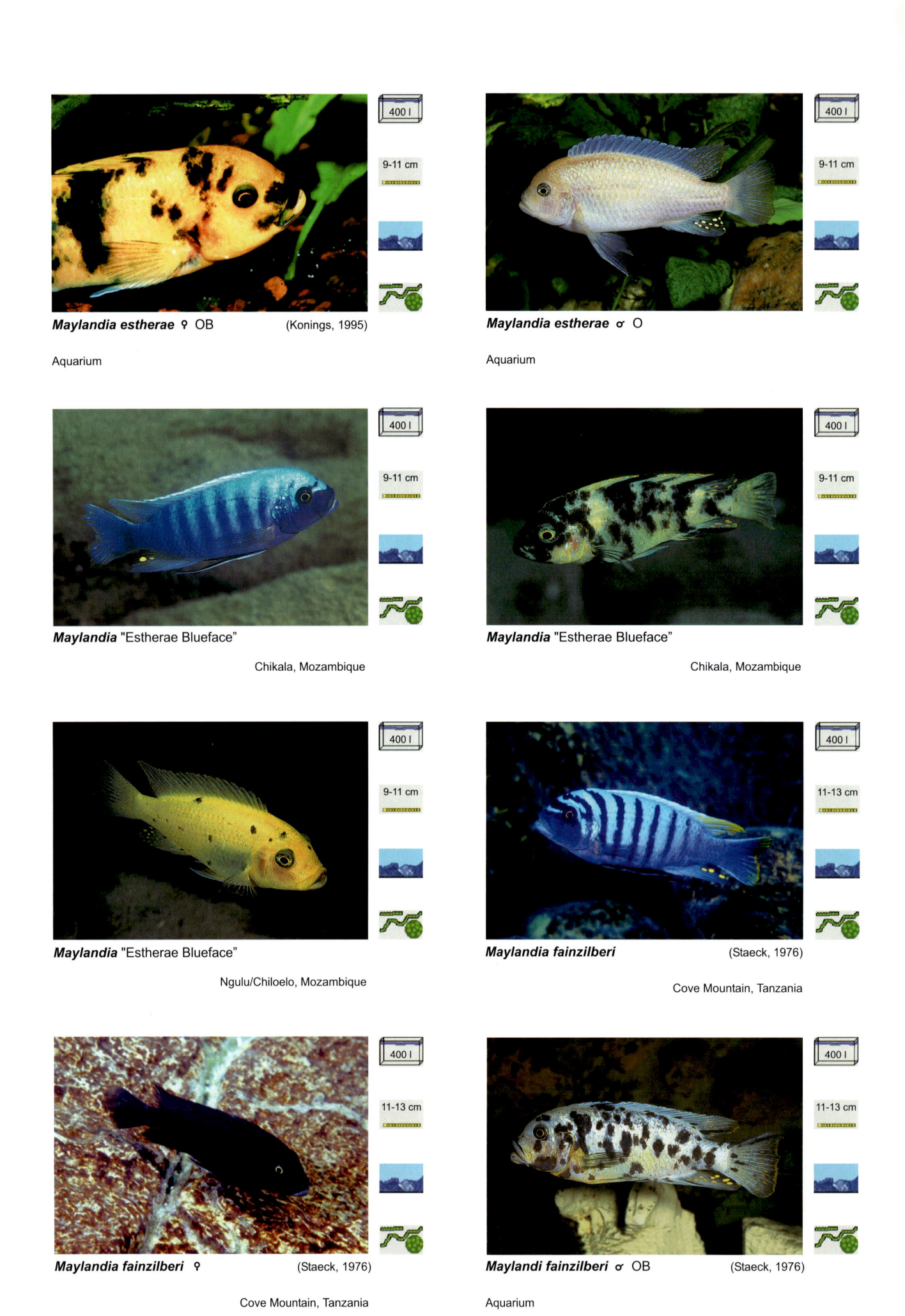

Maylandia estherae ♀ OB   (Konings, 1995)

Aquarium

Maylandia estherae ♂ O

Aquarium

Maylandia "Estherae Blueface"

Chikala, Mozambique

Maylandia "Estherae Blueface"

Chikala, Mozambique

Maylandia "Estherae Blueface"

Ngulu/Chiloelo, Mozambique

Maylandia fainzilberi   (Staeck, 1976)

Cove Mountain, Tanzania

Maylandia fainzilberi ♀   (Staeck, 1976)

Cove Mountain, Tanzania

Maylandi fainzilberi ♂ OB   (Staeck, 1976)

Aquarium

34

Maylandia greshakei (Meyer & Förster, 1984)

Makokola Reef, Malawi

Maylandia greshakei ♀ (Meyer & Förster, 1984)

Aquarium   Makokola-Reef-Population, Malawi

Maylandia greshakei (Meyer & Förster, 1984)

Fotobecken   Makokola Reef, Malawi

Maylandia mbenji (Stauffer et al.,1997)
(ex: Pseudotropheus "Zebra Mbenji")

Mbenji Island, Malawi

Maylandia mbenji ♂ OB (Stauffer et al.,1997)
(ex: Pseudotropheus "Zebra Mbenji")

Mbenji Island, Malawi

Maylandia pyrsonotus (Stauffer et al.,1997)
(ex: Pseudotropheus "Zebra Red Dorsal")

Nakanthenga Island, Malawi

Maylandia pyrsonotus ♂ O (Stauffer et al.,1997)
(ex: Pseudotropheus "Zebra Red Dorsal")
Aquarium

Maylandia pyrsonotus ♂ O (Stauffer et al.,1997)
(ex: Pseudotropheus "Zebra Red Dorsal")
Aquarium

Maylandia xanstomachus (Stauffer & Boltz, 1989)

Aquarium

Maylandia xanstomachus ♂+♀ OB (Stauffer & Boltz, 1989)

Aquarium

Maylandia xanstomachus (Stauffer & Boltz, 1989)

Nakanthenga Island., Malawi

Maylandia zebra (Boulenger, 1899)

Boadzulu Island, Malawi

Maylandia zebra (Boulenger, 1899)

Thumbi West Island, Malawi

Maylandia zebra (Boulenger, 1899)

Membe Point/Likoma Island, Malawi

Maylandia zebra (Boulenger, 1899)

Chiwe Rocks/Chisumulu Island, Malawi

Maylandia zebra ♂ O (Boulenger, 1899)

Lundo Island, Tanzania

Maylandia zebra (Boulenger, 1899)

Ponta Messuli, Mozambique

Maylandia zebra (Boulenger, 1899)

Tumbi Rocks, Tanzania

Maylandia zebra (Boulenger, 1899)

Cove Mountain, Tanzania

Maylandia "Zebra Blue"

Maleri Island, Malawi

Maylandia "Zebra Chilumba"

Aquarium Chilumba-Population, Malawi

Maylandia "Zebra Chilumba"

Chitendi Island/Chilumba, Malawi

Maylandia "Zebra Gold"

Nkhata Bay, Malawi

Maylandia "Zebra Gold"

Lions Cove, Malawi

37

Maylandia "Zebra Goldbreast"

Mara Rocks/Usisya, Malawi

Maylandia "Zebra Goldbreast Mbamba"

Ngkuyo Island/Mbamba Bay, Tanzania

Maylandia "Zebra Goldbreast Mozambique" ♀

N'nosi Reef/Miluluka, Mozambique

Maylandia "Zebra Goldbreast Mozambique"

N'nosi Reef/Miluluka, Mozambique

Maylandia "Zebra Goldbreast Mozambique"

Chikala, Mozambique

Maylandia "Zebra Goldbreast Mozambique"

Jilambo, Mozambique

Maylandia "Zebra Goldbreast Orange Top"

Lundo Island, Tanzania

Maylandia "Zebra Goldbreast Orange Top"

Puulu Island, Tanzania

Maylandia "Zebra Mbamba Bay Kompakt"

Ngkuyo Island/Mbamba Bay, Tanzania

Maylandia "Zebra Mbamba Bay Kompakt"

Mara Rocks/Mbamba Bay, Tanzania

Maylandia "Zebra Mbamba Bay Kompakt" ♂ OB

Ngkuyo Island/Mbamba Bay, Tanzania

Maylandia "Zebra Mbamba Bay Kompakt" ♀ OB

Ngkuyo Island/Mbamba Bay, Tanzania

Maylandia "Zebra Mozambique"

Gome Rock/Makanjila, Mozambique

Maylandia "Zebra South"

Hai Reef, Tanzania

Maylandia "Zebra South"

Hai Reef, Tanzania

Maylandia "Zebra South"

Ponta Messuli, Mozambique

39

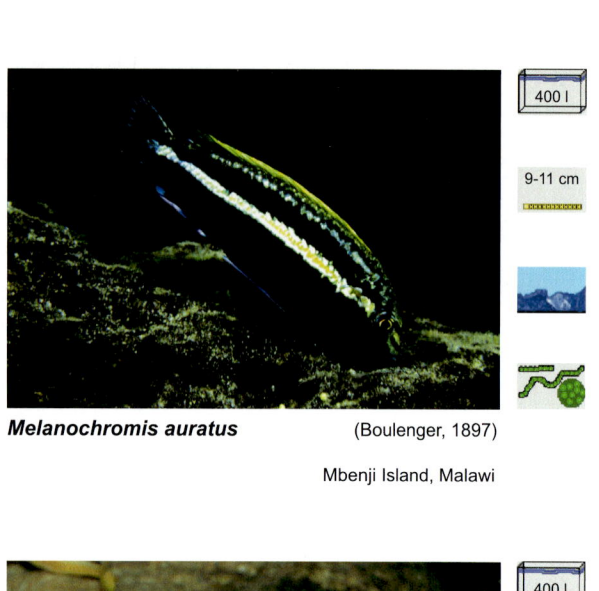

Melanochromis auratus (Boulenger, 1897)

Mbenji Island, Malawi

Melanochromis auratus ♀ (Boulenger, 1897)

Nakanthenga Island Malawi

Melanochromis auratus, Jungtiere

Aquarium

Melanochromis "Auratus Elongate"

Chuanga/Metangula, Mozambique

Melanochromis "Auratus Elongate"

Chuanga/Metangula, Mozambique

Melanochromis "Auratus Elongate" ♀

Chuanga/Metangula, Mozambique

Melanochromis baliodigma (Bowers & Stauffer, 1997)
(ex: *Melanochromis* "Blotch")

Chisumulu-Population/Chisumulu Island, Malawi

Melanochromis baliodigma (Bowers & Stauffer, 1997)
(ex: *Melanochromis* "Blotch")

Chisumulu-Population/Chisumulu Island, Malawi

Melanochromis benetos Bowers & Stauffer, 1997
(ex: *Melanochromis* "Blue")
Chirwa Island/Chilumba, Malawi

Melanochromis benetos ♀ Bowers & Stauffer, 1997
(ex: *Melanochromis* "Blue")
Ngkuyo Island/Mbamba Bay, Tanzania

Melanochromis benetos Bowers & Stauffer, 1997
(ex: *Melanochromis* "Blue")
Chirwa Island/Chilumba, Malawi

Melanochromis benetos Bowers & Stauffer, 1997
(ex: *Melanochromis* "Blue")
Aquarium   Chinula-Population/Mbamba Bay, Tanzania

Melanochromis cf. brevis Trewavas, 1935
Chinyankhwazi Island, Malawi

Melanochromis cyaneorhabdos Bowers & Stauffer,
(ex: *Melanochromis* "Maingano")   1997
Maingano/Likoma Island, Malawi

Melanochromis dialeptos Bowers & Stauffer, 1997
(ex: *Melanochromis* "Auratus Dwarf")
Aquarium

Melanochromis dialeptos ♀ Bowers & Stauffer, 1997
(ex: *Melanochromis* "Auratus Dwarf")
Aquarium

Melanochromis dialeptos Bowers & Stauffer, 1997
(ex: *Melanochromis* "Auratus Dwarf")
Chikala, Mozambique

Melanochromis dialeptos ♀ Bowers & Stauffer, 1997
(ex: *Melanochromis* "Auratus Dwarf")
Chikala, Mozambique

Melanochromis interruptus (Johnson, 1975)
(Syn.: *M. elastodema* Bowers & Stauffer, 1997)
Chisumulu Island, Malawi

Melanochromis interruptus ♀ (Johnson, 1975)
(Syn.: *M. elastodema* Bowers & Stauffer, 1997)
Chisumulu Island, Malawi

Melanochromis joanjohnsonae (Johnson, 1974)
Aquarium

Melanochromis joanjohnsonae ♀ (Johnson, 1974)
Aquarium

Melanochromis johannii Eccles, 1973
Aquarium

Melanochromis johannii ♀ Eccles, 1973
Aquarium

Melanochromis johannii Eccles, 1973

Melanochromis johannii jun. Männchen Eccles, 1973

Nyamizimu/Meponda, Mozambique

Melanochromis labrosus Trewavas, 1935
Aquarium

Melanochromis labrosus ♀ Trewavas, 1935
Aquarium

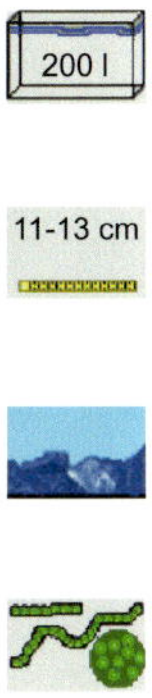

Melanochromis lepidiadaptes Bowers & Stauffer, 1997
(ex: *Melanochromis* "Lepidophage")
Aquarium

Melanochromis lepidiadaptes ♀ Bowers & Stauffer, 1997
(ex: *Melanochromis* "Lepidophage")
Aquarium

Melanochromis loriae Johnson, 1975
Aquarium   Chidunga-Rocks-Population, Chipoka, Malawi

Melanochromis loriae ♀ Johnson, 1975
Fotobecken   Chidunga-Rocks/Chipoka, Malawi

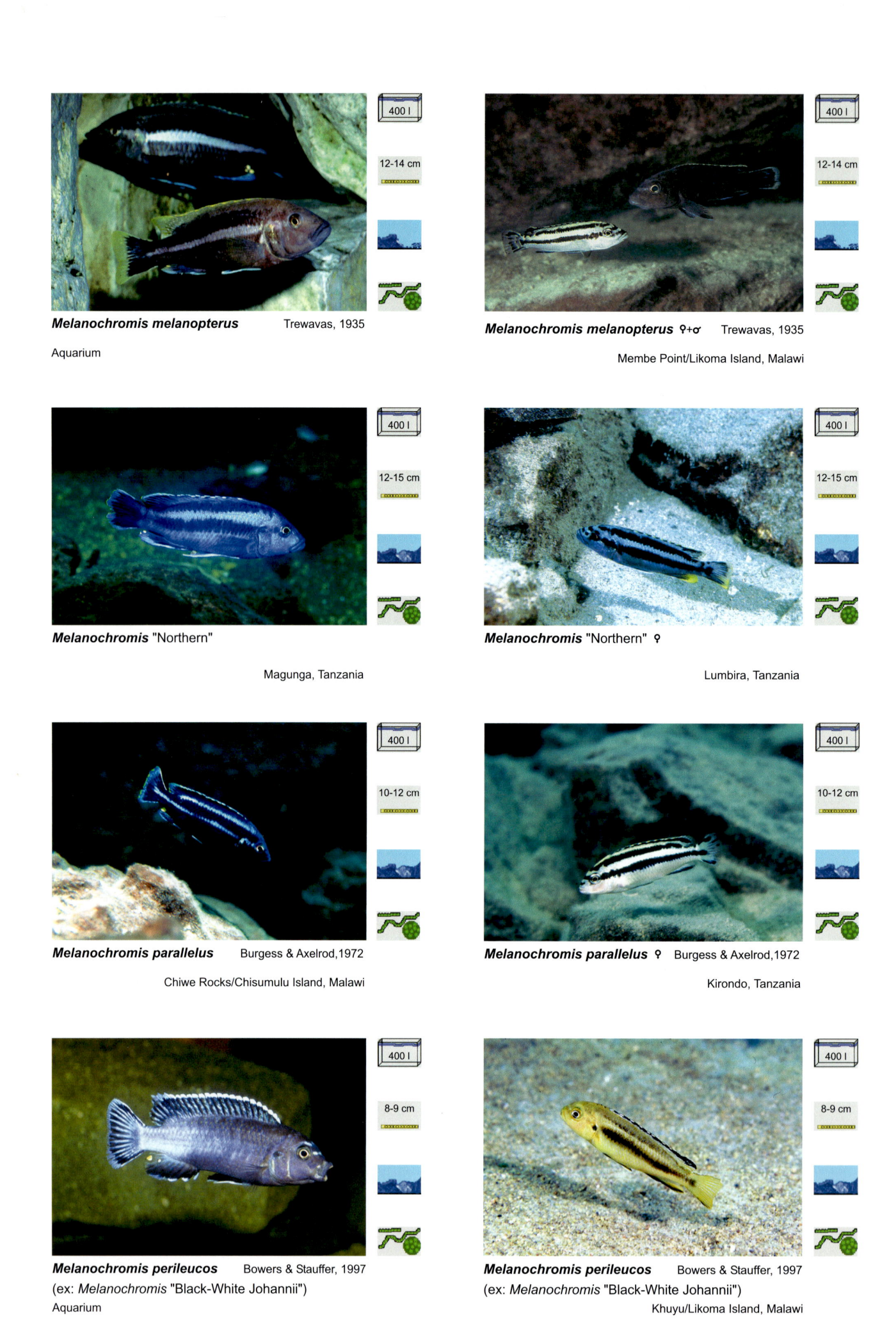

Melanochromis melanopterus   Trewavas, 1935

Aquarium

Melanochromis melanopterus ♀+♂   Trewavas, 1935

Membe Point/Likoma Island, Malawi

Melanochromis "Northern"

Magunga, Tanzania

Melanochromis "Northern" ♀

Lumbira, Tanzania

Melanochromis parallelus   Burgess & Axelrod, 1972

Chiwe Rocks/Chisumulu Island, Malawi

Melanochromis parallelus ♀   Burgess & Axelrod, 1972

Kirondo, Tanzania

Melanochromis perileucos   Bowers & Stauffer, 1997
(ex: *Melanochromis* "Black-White Johannii")
Aquarium

Melanochromis perileucos   Bowers & Stauffer, 1997
(ex: *Melanochromis* "Black-White Johannii")
Khuyu/Likoma Island, Malawi

Melanochromis simulans Eccles, 1973

Aquarium

Melanochromis simulans ♀ Eccles, 1973

Aquarium

Melanochromis "Slab"

Aquarium   Mbenji-Island-Population, Malawi

Melanochromis "Slab" ♀

Aquarium   Mbenji-Island-Population, Malawi

Melanochromis vermivorus Trewavas, 1935

Fotobecken   Mumbo Island, Malawi

Melanochromis vermivorus ♀ Trewavas, 1935

Fotobecken

Melanochromis xanthodigma Bowers & Stauffer, 1997

Nyamizimu/Meponda, Mozambique

Melanochromis xanthodigma Bowers & Stauffer, 1997

Nyamizimu/Meponda, Mozambique

45

Petrotilapia "Black Flank"

Chitendi Island/Chilumba, Malawi

Petrotilapia "Chitande"

Chewere/Chilumba, Malawi

Petrotilapia chrysos   Stauffer & van Snik, 1996
(ex: *Petrotilapia* "Gold")

Chinyamwezi Island, Malawi

Petrotilapia chrysos   Stauffer & van Snik, 1996
(ex: *Petrotilapia* "Gold")

Chinyamwezi Island, Malawi

Petrotilapia "Fuscous"

Nakanthenga Island, Malawi

Petrotilapia genalutea   Marsh, 1983

Maleri Island, Malawi

Petrotilapia "Gold Eastern"

Nyamizimu/Meponda, Mozambique

Petrotilapia "Gold Eastern"

Gome Rock/Makanjila, Malawi

Petrotilapia "Likoma Barred"

Mazimbwe Island/Likoma Island, Malawi

Petrotilapia "Likoma Barred"

Msekwa Point/Likoma Island, Malawi

Petrotilapia "Likoma Variable" ♀

Mazimbwe Island/Likoma Island, Malawi

Petrotilapia "Likoma Variable"

Mazimbwe Island/Likoma Island, Malawi

Petrotilapia "Mumbo Yellow"

Mumbo Island, Malawi

Petrotilapia "Mumbo Blue"

Mumbo Island, Malawi

Petrotilapia nigra Marsh, 1983

Thumbi West Island, Malawi

Petrotilapia nigra Marsh, 1983

Thumbi West Island, Malawi

Petrotilapia "Nigra Tumbi" ♀

Tumbi Point, Mozambique

Petrotilapia "Nigra Tumbi"

Mara Point/Cobue, Mozambique

Petrotilapia "Orange Pelvic"

Membe Island/Chisumulu Island, Malawi

Petrotilapia "Pointed Head"

Undu Point, Tanzania

Petrotilapia "Retrognathus"

Membe Island/Chisumulu Island, Malawi

Petrotilapia "Ruarwe"

Chitendi Island/Chisumulu Island, Malawi

Petrotilapia "Small Blue"

Nkhata Bay, Malawi

Petrotilapia "Small Blue" ♀

Nkhata Bay, Malawi

Petrotilapia "Tanzania"

Magunga, Tanzania

Petrotilapia "Tanzania"

Manda, Tanzania

Petrotilapia tridentiger   Trewavas, 1935

Chilumba, Malawi

Petrotilapia tridentiger ♀   Trewavas, 1935

Chilumba, Malawi

Petrotilapia "Yellow Chin"

Aquarium   Maleri-Island-Population, Malawi

Petrotilapia "Yellow Chin" ♀

Aquarium   Maleri-Island-Population, Malawi

Petrotilapia "Yellow Ventral"

Chilanje/Chisumulu Island, Malawi

Petrotilapia "Yellow Ventral"

Aquarium

Pseudotropheus "Acei"

Aquarium Nkhata-Bay-Population, Malawi

Pseudotropheus "Acei"

Aquarium Kambiri-Population, Malawi

Pseudotropheus "Acei"

Aquarium Ngara-Population, Malawi

Pseudotropheus "Aggressive Grey"

Ndomo Point/Likoma Island, Malawi

Pseudotropheus "Aggressive Puulu"

Puulu, Tanzania

Pseudotropheus "Aggressive Yellow Fin"

Chisumulu Island., Malawi

Pseudotropheus "Aggressive Yellow Head"

Nakanthenga Island., Malawi

Pseudotropheus "Aggressive Zebra"

Ndomo Point/Likoma Island, Malawi

Pseudotropheus aurora Burgess, 1976

Chiponde/Likoma Island, Malawi

Pseudotropheus aurora ♀ Burgess, 1976

Khuyu/Likoma Island, Malawi

Pseudotropheus "Aurora Blue"
(ex: *Pseudotropheus* "Zebra Blue Reef")
Kanjindo/Cobué, Mocambique

Pseudotropheus "Aurora Blue"
(ex: *Pseudotropheus* "Zebra Blue Reef")
Namisi Rock/Cobué, Mozambique

Pseudotropheus "Aurora Uchesi"

Uchesi Rocks/Cobué, Mozambique

Pseudotropheus "Aurora Uchesi" ♀

Uchesi Rocks/Cobué, Mozambique

Pseudotropheus barlowi McKaye & Stauffer, 1966

Aquarium   Mbenji-Population

Pseudotropheus barlowi McKaye & Stauffer, 1986

Nakanthenga Island, Malawi

Pseudotropheus "Black Dorsal"

Maleri Island., Malawi

Pseudotropheus "Black Dorsal"

Thumbi West Island, Malawi

Pseudotropheus "Black Dorsal Chiloelo"

Jilambo, Mozambique

Pseudotropheus "Black Dorsal Londo"   (Stauffer et al.,
(= ? *Pseudotropheus phaeos*)   1997)

Londo/Ponta Messuli, Mozambique

Pseudotropheus "Black Dorsal Londo" ♀ (Stauffer et al.,
(= ? *Pseudotropheus phaeos*)   1997)

Londo/Ponta Messuli, Mozambique

Pseudotropheus "Black Dorsal Tanzania"

Undu Point, Tanzania

Pseudotropheus "Black Dorsal Tanzania" ♀

Undu Point, Tanzania

Pseudotropheus "Black Dorsal Nkolongwe"

Aquarium   Nkolongwe-Population, Mozambique

Pseudotropheus "Broad Bar"

Lundu, Tanzania

Pseudotropheus spec. "Burrower"

Aquarium — Nakanthenga-Island-Population, Malawi

Pseudotropheus crabro (Ribbink & Lewis, 1982)

Aquarium — Mbenji-Island-Population, Malawi

Pseudotropheus crabro ♀ (Ribbink & Lewis, 1982)

Mbamba Bay, Tanzania

Pseudotropheus "Daktari"

Hai Reef, Tanzania

Pseudotropheus "Daktari"

Aquarium — Mozambique-Population

Pseudotropheus demasoni Konings, 1994

Aquarium — Pombo-Rocks-Population, Tanzania

Pseudotropheus "Dolphin"

Puulu, Tanzania

Pseudotropheus elegans Trewavas, 1935

Fotobecken Senga Bay, Malawi

Pseudotropheus hajomaylandi Meyer & Schartl, 1984

Fotobecken Chisumulu Island, Malawi

Pseudotropheus heteropictus Staeck, 1980

Chisumulu Isl., Malawi

Pseudotropheus heteropictus ♀ Staeck, 1980

Chisumulu Island, Malawi

Pseudotropheus "Jacksoni"

Aquarium

Pseudotropheus "Kingsizei"

Maingano/Likoma Island, Malawi

Pseudotropheus "Kingsizei"

Ponta Messuli, Mozambique

Pseudotropheus livingstonii (Boulenger, 1899)

Aquarium

54

Pseudotropheus "Livingstonii Likoma"

Makulawe Point/Likoma Island, Malawi

Pseudotropheus lombardoi Burgess, 1977

Aquarium Mbenji-Island-Population, Malawi

Pseudotropheus lombardoi ♀ Burgess, 1977

Aquarium Mbenji-Island-Population, Malawi

Pseudotropheus "Membe Deep"

Membe Point/Likoma Island, Malawi

Pseudotropheus minutus Fryer, 1956

Aquarium Nkhata-Bay-Population, Malawi

Pseudotropheus minutus ♀ Fryer, 1956

Aquarium Nkhata-Bay-Population, Malawi

Pseudotropheus "Msobo"

Magunga, Tanzania

Pseudotropheus "Msobo" ♀

Magunga, Tanzania

Pseudotropheus "Msobo"

Puulu, Tanzania

Pseudotropheus "Msobo"

Aquarium   Lundo-Island-Population, Tanzania

Pseudotropheus "Ndumbi Gold"

Aquarium   Ndumbi-Rocks-Population/Likoma Island, Malawi

Pseudotropheus "Ndumbi Gold" ♀

Ndumbi Rocks/Likoma Island, Malawi

Pseudotropheus "Orange Cap"

Undu Point, Tanzania

Pseudotropheus "Patricki"

Mbenji Isl., Malawi

Pseudotropheus "Patricki"

Fotobecken   Mbenji Island, Malawi

Pseudotropheus "Plain"

Kirondo, Tanzania

Pseudotropheus "Polit"

Lions Cove, Malawi

Pseudotropheus "Pombo Yellow Breast"

Pombo Rocks, Tanzania

Pseudotropheus "Red Dorsal"

Aquarium   Mbenji-Island-Population, Malawi

Pseudotropheus "Red Top Ndumbi"

Ndumbi Reef, Tanzania

Pseudotropheus saulosi   Konings, 1990

Taiwan Reef/Chisumulu Island, Malawi

Pseudotropheus saulosi ♀   Konings, 1990

Taiwan Reef/Chisumulu Island, Malawi

Pseudotropheus socolofi   Johnson, 1990

Mara Point/Cobué, Mozambique

Pseudotropheus "Tiny"

Thumbi West Island, Malawi

Pseudotropheus tursiops Burgess & Axelrod, 1975

Ikombe, Tanzania

Pseudotropheus tursiops ♀ Burgess & Axelrod, 1975

Chirwa Island/Chilumba, Malawi

Pseudotropheus "Tursiops Mbenji"

Mbenji Island, Malawi

Pseudotropheus "Variable Tanzania"

Puulu, Tanzania

Pseudotropheus williamsi (Günther, 1893)

Mbenji Island., Malawi

Pseudotropheus williamsi (Günther, 1893)

Nakanthenga Island, Malawi

Pseudotropheus williamsi (Günther, 1893)

Aquarium

Pseudotropheus williamsi (Günther, 1893)

Aquarium   Population nördl. Manda, Tanzania

Pseudotropheus "Zebra Bevous"

Membe Island/Chisumulu Island, Malawi

Pseudotropheus "Zebra Blue Gold"

Lupingu, Tanzania

Pseudotropheus "Zebra Masinje"

Fort Maguire, Malawi

Pseudotropheus "Zebra Slim"

Magunga, Tanzania

Pseudotropheus "Zebra Slim"

Nkanda, Tanzania

Pseudotropheus "Zebra Yellow Belly"

Ndumbi Reef, Tanzania

Pseudotropheus "Zebra Yellow Belly" ♀

Ndumbi Reef, Tanzania

Pseudotropheus "Zebra Yellow Tail"
(= *Pseudotropheus* "Yellow Tail" leg. Spreinat, 1994)

Cove Moutain/Manda, Tanzania

Pseudotropheus ater (semiadult) Stauffer, 1983

Chinyamwezi Island, Malawi

Pseudotropheus ater Stauffer, 1983

Chinyamwezi Island, Malawi

Pseudotropheus cyaneus Stauffer, 1983

Chinyamwezi Island, Malawi

Pseudotropheus cyaneus Stauffer, 1983

Chinyamwezi Island., Malawi

Pseudotropheus elongatus Fryer, 1956
(ex: *Pseudotropheus* "Elongatus Sand")
Mara Rocks/Mbamba Bay, Tanzania

Pseudotropheus elongatus ♀ Fryer, 1956
(ex: *Pseudotropheus* "Elongatus Sand")
Mara Rocks/Mbamba Bay, Tanzania

Pseudotropheus elongatus Fryer, 1956
(ex: *Pseudotropheus* "Elongatus Sand")
Aquarium   Chinula-Population/Mbamba Bay, Tanzania

Pseudotropheus elongatus ♀ Fryer, 1956
(ex: *Pseudotropheus* "Elongatus Sand")
Aquarium   Chinula-Population/Mbamba Bay, Tanzania

Pseudotropheus "Elongatus Aggressive"

Thumbi West Island, Malawi

Pseudotropheus "Elongatus Aggressive"

Mumbo Island., Malawi

Pseudotropheus "Elongatus Bar"

Maleri Island, Malawi

Pseudotropheus "Elongatus Bee"

Chitendi Island/Chilumba, Malawi

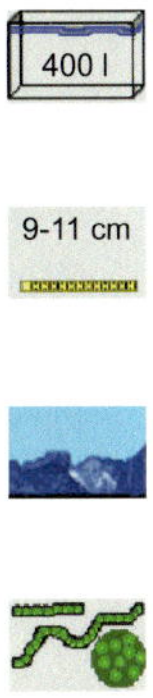

Pseudotropheus "Elongatus Boadzulu"

Boadzulu Island, Malawi

Pseudotropheus "Elongatus Chewere"

Chewere/Chilumba, Malawi

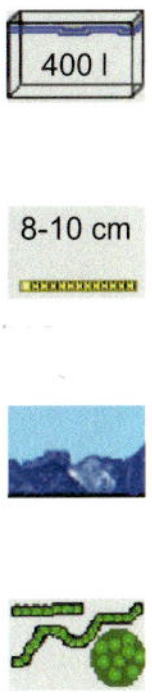

Pseudotropheus "Elongatus Chisumulu"

Membe Island/Chisumulu Island, Malawi

Pseudotropheus "Elongatus Deep Water"

Ngkuyo Isl./Mbamba Bay, Tanzania

Pseudotropheus "Elongatus Gold Bar"

Chilanje/Chisumulu Island, Malawi

Pseudotropheus "Elongatus Luhuchi"

Luhuchi Rocks/Mbamba Bay, Tanzania

Pseudotropheus "Elongatus Luhuchi" ♀

Luhuchi Rocks/Mbamba Bay, Tanzania

Pseudotropheus "Elongatus Mazimbwe"

Mazimbwe/Likoma Island, Malawi

Pseudotropheus "Elongatus Mbako"

Maingano/Likoma Island, Malawi

Pseudotropheus "Elongatus Mbenji Blue"

Mbenji Island, Malawi

Pseudotropheus "Elongatus Metangula"

Lingwezi, Mozambique

Pseudotropheus "Elongatus Mpanga"

Mpanga Rocks/Chilumba, Malawi

Pseudotropheus "Elongatus Namalenji"

Namalenji Island, Malawi

Pseudotropheus "Elongatus Ngkuyo"

Ngkuyo Island/Mbamba Bay, Tanzania

Pseudotropheus "Elongatus Ngkuyo"

Higga Reef/Mbamba Bay, Tanzania

Pseudotropheus "Elongatus Nkhata Brown"

Chikale/Nkhata Bay, Malawi

Pseudotropheus "Elongatus Ornatus" ♀

Aquarium   Likoma-Island-Population, Malawi

Pseudotropheus "Elongatus Ornatus"

Ndumbi Rocks/Likoma Island, Malawi

Pseudotropheus "Elongatus Reef"

Eccles Reef, Malawi

Pseudotropheus "Elongatus Slab"

Makokola Reef, Malawi

63

Pseudotropheus "Elongatus Spot"

Aquarium Lundo-Island-Population, Tanzania

Pseudotropheus "Elongatus Usisya"

Aquarium Mara-Rocks-Population, Malawi

Pseudotropheus "Elongatus Usisya"

Mara Rocks/Usisya, Malawi

Pseudotropheus "Elongatus Yellow Tail"

Mumbo Island, Malawi

Pseudotropheus flavus Stauffer, 1983

Chinyankhwazi Island, Malawi

Pseudotropheus flavus ♀

Aquarium

Pseudotropheus longior Seegers, 1996
(ex: *Pseudotropheus* "Elongatus Mbamba")

Pseudotropheus "Elongatus Mbamba" ♀ Seegers, 1996
(ex: *Pseudotropheus* "Elongatus Mbamba")

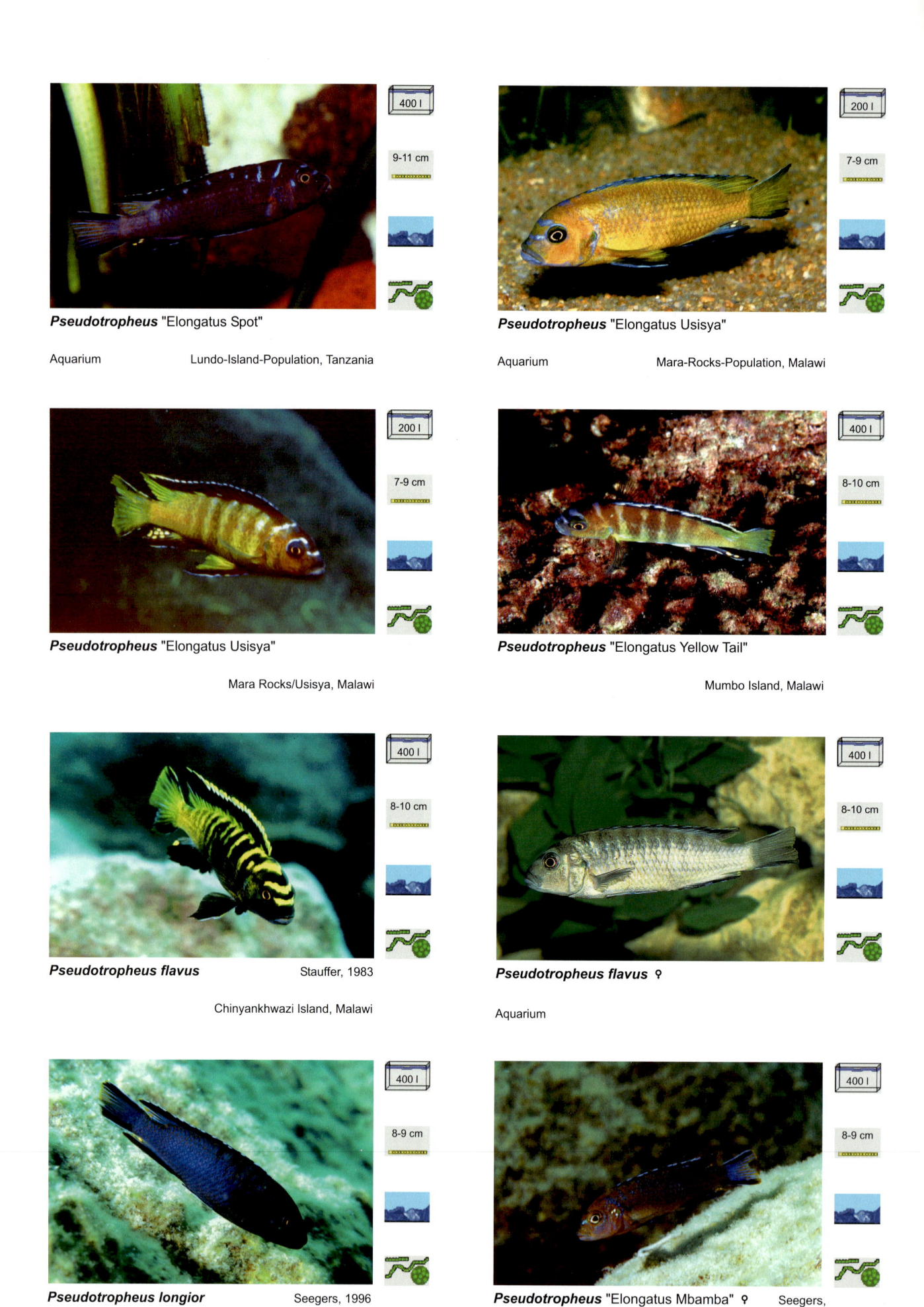

Tropheops "Black"

Mpanga Rock/Chilumba, Malawi

Tropheops "Boadzulu"

Boadzulu Island., Malawi

Tropheops "Checkered"

Ikombe, Tanzania

Tropheops " Checkered" ♀

Lumbira, Tanzania

Tropheops "Chilumba"

Aquarium Chilumba-Population, Malawi

Tropheops "Chilumba" ♀

Aquarium Chilumba-Population, Malawi

Tropheops "Chilumba"

Aquarium Chilumba-Population, Malawi

Tropheops "Lilac Mumbo"

Mumbo Island, Malawi

65

Tropheops "Mauve"

Chirwa Island., Malawi

Tropheops "Mauve" ♀

Usisya, Malawi

Tropheops " Mbamba"

Puulu, Tanzania

Tropheops "Mbamba" ♀

Puulu, Tanzania

Tropheops "Membe"

Mara Point/Cobué, Mozambique

Tropheops "Mumbo"

Mumbo Island, Malawi

Tropheops "Mutant"

Cove Mountain/Manda, Tanzania

Tropheops "Olive"

Mpanga Rocks/Chilumba, Malawi

Tropheops "Orange Chest"
(= ? Tropheops tropheops)
Boadzulu Island, Malawi

Tropheops "Orange Chest"
(= ? Tropheops tropheops)
Tsano Rock/Monkey Bay, Malawi

Tropheops "Red Cheek"
Thumbi West Island, Malawi

Tropheops "Red Cheek" ♀
Thumbi West Island, Malawi

Tropheops "Red Fin"
(= ? Tropheops gracilior)
Aquarium Ruarwe-Population, Malawi

Tropheops "Red Fin" ♀
(= ? Tropheops gracilior)
Aquarium Ruarwe-Population, Malawi

Tropheops "Red Fin" ♀
(= ? Tropheops gracilior)
Londo, Mozambique

Tropheops "Red Fin" ♀
(= ? Tropheops gracilior)
Puulu Island, Tanzania

Tropheops "Rusty Hongi"

Hongi Island, Tanzania

Tropheops "Sand"

Nkanda, Tanzania

Tropheops "Sand" ♀

Nkanda, Tanzania

Tropheops "Weed"

Chewere/Chilumba, Malawi

Tropheops "Weed"

Lundo Island, Tanzania

Tropheops "Weed" ♀

Lundo Island, Tanzania

Tropheops "Yellow Chin"

Membe Island/Chisumulu Island, Malawi

Tropheops "Yellow Head"

Undu Point, Tanzania

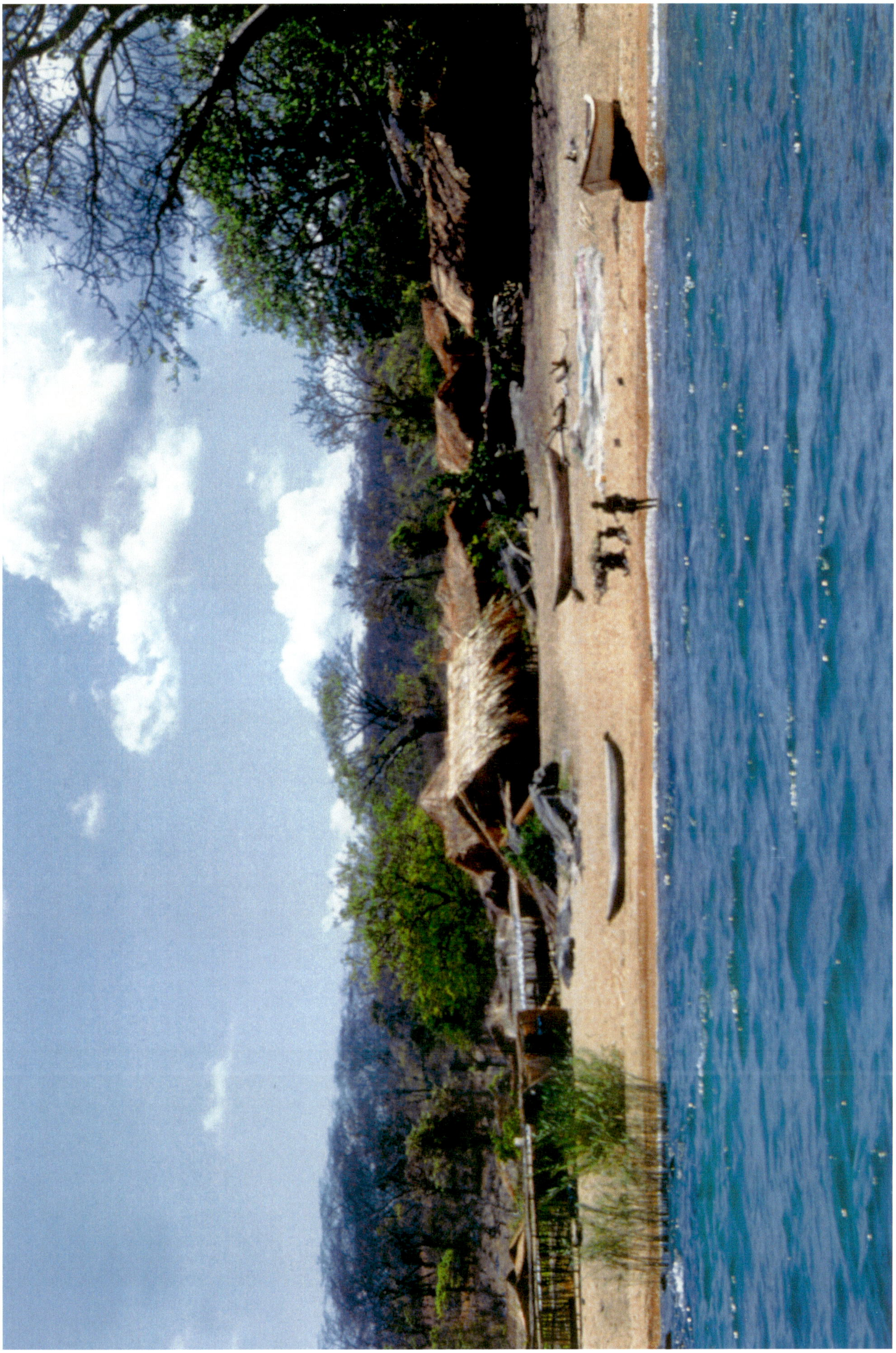

Alticorpus mentale   Stauffer & McKaye, 1988

Makanjila, Malawi

Aristochromis christyi   Trewavas, 1935

Aquarium

Aristochromis christyi ♀   Trewavas, 1935

Aquarium

Aristochromis christyi   Trewavas, 1935

Aquarium

Aulonocara baenschi   Meyer & Riehl, 1985

Aquarium   Benga-Population, Malawi

Aulonocara baenschi ♀   Meyer & Riehl, 1985

Aquarium   Benga-Population, Malawi

Aulonocara baenschi

Fotobecken   Benga, Malawi

Aulonocara baenschi   Meyer & Riehl, 1985

Aquarium   Benga-Population, Malawi

Aulonocara baenschi Meyer & Riehl, 1985

Aquarium Maleri-Island-Population, Malawi

Aulonocara baenschi Meyer & Riehl, 1985

Fotobecken Chipoka, Malawi

Aulonocara baenschi Meyer & Riehl, 1985

Aquarium Chipoka-Population, Malawi

Aulonocara baenschi Meyer & Riehl, 1985

Zuchtform Chipoka-Population, Malawi

Aulonocara "Black Top"

Masimbwe/Likoma Island, Malawi

Aulonocara "Black Top" ♀

Masimbwe/Likoma Island, Malawi

Aulonocara "Black Top"

Makulawe Point/Likoma Island, Malawi

Aulonocara "Black Top"

Chiteko/Chisumulu

Aulonocara brevinidus Konings, 1995

Lupono/Mbamba Bay, Tanzania

Aulonocara brevinidus Konings, 1995

Aquarium

Aulonocara "Chitendi Type East Coast"

Aquarium Masinje-Population, Malawi

Aulonocara "Chitendi Type East Coast" ♀

Aquarium Masinje-Population, Malawi

Aulonocara "Chitendi Type East Coast"

Masinje/Makanjila, Malawi

Aulonocara "Chitendi Type East Coast"

Londo, Mozambique

Aulonocara "Cobue"

Namisi Rock/Cobué, Mozambique

Aulonocara "Cobue"

Fotobecken Thumbi West Island, Malawi

Aulonocara ethelwynnae Meyer, Riehl & Zetzsche, 1987
Chitendi Island/Chilumba, Malawi

Aulonocara ethelwynnae Meyer, Riehl & Zetzsche, 1987
Chitendi Island/Chilumba, Malawi

Aulonocara gertrudae Konings, 1995
Aquarium

Aulonocara gertrudae ♀ Konings, 1995
Aquarium

Aulonocara guentheri Eccles, 1989
Senga Bay, Malawi

Aulonocara guentheri ♀ Eccles, 1989
Senga Bay, Malawi

Aulonocara hansbaens Meyer, Riehl & Zetzsche, 1987
Aquarium   Makanjila, Malawi

Aulonocara hansbaenschi ♀ Meyer, Riehl & Zetzsche, 1987
Makanjila, Malawi

Aulonocara hansbaenschi   Meyer, Riehl & Zetzsche, 1987
Ngumbe Rock/Minga Bay, Mozambique

Aulonocara hansbaenschi ♀   Meyer, Riehl & Zetzsche, 1987
Ngumbe Rock/Minga Bay, Mozambique

Aulonocara hueseri   Meyer, Riehl & Zetzsche, 1987
Aquarium   Likoma-Island-Population, Malawi

Aulonocara hueseri   Meyer, Riehl & Zetzsche, 1987
Mbuzi Island/Likoma Island, Malawi

Aulonocara jacobfreibergi   (Johnson, 1974)
Fotobecken   Cape Maclear, Malawi

Aulonocara jacobfreibergi   (Johnson, 1974)
Tsano Rock/Monkey Bay, Malawi

Aulonocara jacobfreibergi ♀   (Johnson, 1974)
Aquarium

Aulonocara jacobfreibergi   (Johnson, 1974)
Zuchtform ("Eureka")
Aquarium

Aulonocara "Kande Brown"

Kande Island, Malawi

Aulonocara "Kande Brown" ♀

Fotobecken   Kande-Island-Population, Malawi

Aulonocara korneliae   Meyer, Riehl & Zetzsche, 1987

Chisumulu Island, Malawi

Aulonocara korneliae   Meyer, Riehl & Zetzsche, 1987

Chisumulu Island, Malawi

Aulonocara "Lupingu"

Makonde, Tanzania

Aulonocara "Lupingu"

Lupingu, Tanzania

Aulonocara "Lupingu"

Lupingu/Tanzania

Aulonocara "Lupingu" ♀

Nkanda/Tanzania

75

Aulonocara "Mamelela"

Aquarium　　　　　　　　　Undu Point, Tanzania

Aulonocara "Mamelela"

　　　　　　　　　　　　　Undu Point, Tanzania

Aulonocara "Mamelela" ♀

Aquarium

Aulonocara "Mamelela"

Aquarium

Aulonocara maylandi　　　Trewavas, 1984

　　　　　　　　　　　　　Eccles Reef, Malawi

Aulonocara maylandi　　　Trewavas, 1984

Aquarium　　　　　　　　　Eccles-Reef-Population, Malawi

Aulonocara kandeensis　　Tawil & Allgayer, 1987
(ex: *A. maylandi kandeensis*)
　　　　　　　　　　　　　Kande Island, Malawi

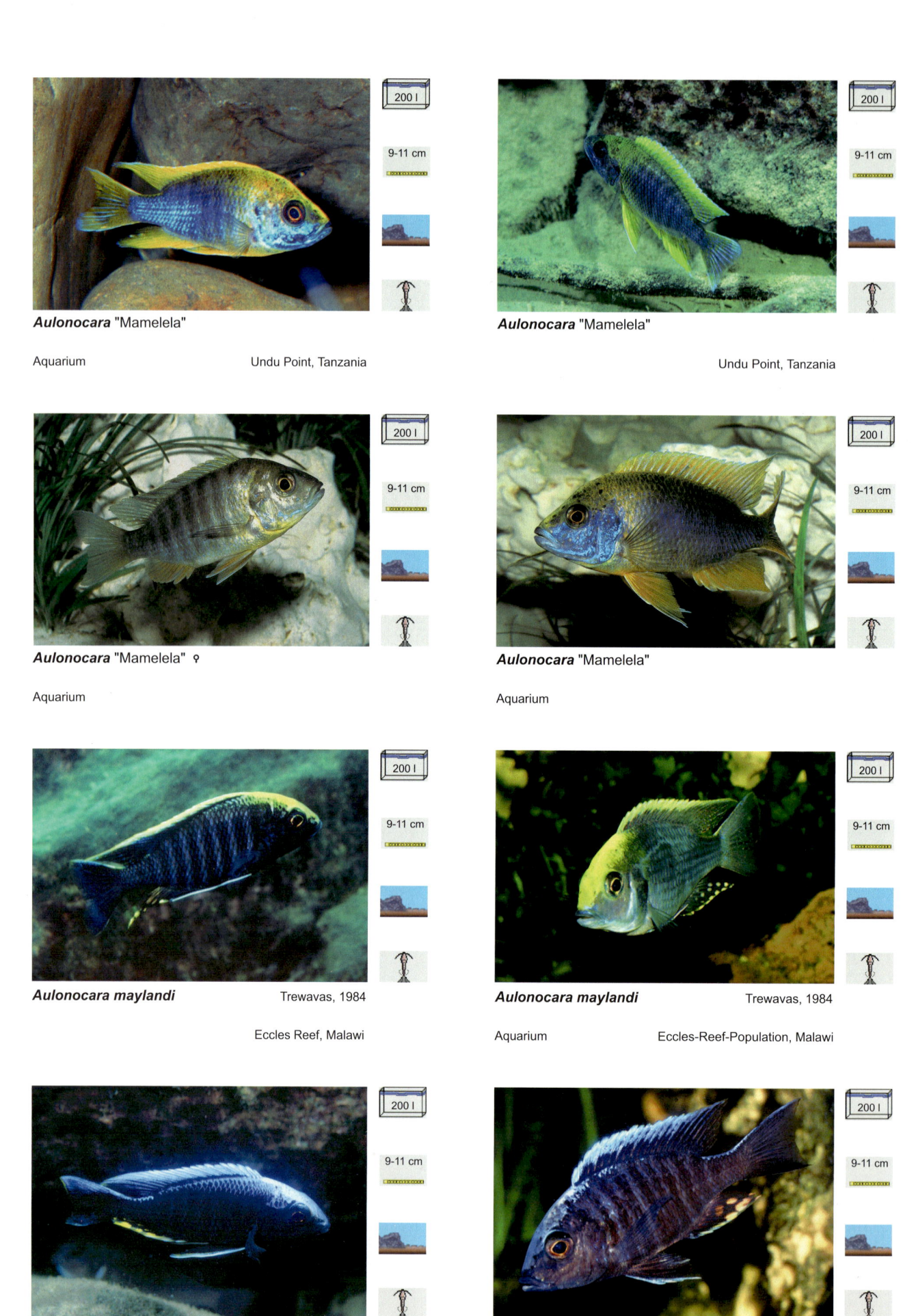

Aulonocara kandeensis　　Tawil & Allgayer, 1987
(ex: *A. maylandi kandeensis*)
Aquarium　　　　　　　　　Kande-Island-Population, Malawi

Aulonocara rostratum Trewavas, 1935

Aquarium

Aulonocara rostratum ♀ Trewavas, 1935

Aquarium

Aulonocara saulosi Meyer, Riehl & Zetzsche, 1987

Aquarium Likoma-Island-Population, Malawi

Aulonocara saulosi ♀ Meyer, Riehl & Zetzsche, 1987

Aquarium Likoma-Island-Population, Malawi

Aulonocara saulosi Meyer, Riehl & Zetzsche, 1987

Likoma-Island, Malawi

Aulonocara steveni Meyer, Riehl & Zetzsche, 1987

Kande-Island, Malawi

Aulonocara steveni Meyer, Riehl & Zetzsche, 1987

Aquarium Usisya-Population, Malawi

Aulonocara steveni ♀ Meyer, Riehl & Zetzsche, 1987

Aquarium Usisya-Population, Malawi

Aulonocara steveni   Meyer, Riehl & Zetzsche, 1987

Aquarium   Usisya-Population, Malawi

Aulonocara steveni   Meyer, Riehl & Zetzsche, 1987

Aquarium   Njambe, Tanzania

Aulonocara steveni   Meyer, Riehl & Zetzsche, 1987

Ponton/Mbamba Bay, Tanzania

Aulonocara steveni   Meyer, Riehl & Zetzsche, 1987

Undu Point, Tanzania

Aulonocara steveni   Meyer, Riehl & Zetzsche, 1987

Hai Reef, Tanzania

Aulonocara stuartgranti   Meyer & Riehl, 1985

Fotobecken   Chilumba, Malawi

Aulonocara stuartgranti   Meyer & Riehl, 1985

Aquarium   Chilumba-Population, Malawi

Aulonocara stuartgranti   Meyer & Riehl, 1985

Aquarium   Chilumba-Population, Malawi

Aulonocara stuartgranti　　　Meyer & Riehl, 1985

Aquarium　　　Ngara-Population, Malawi

Aulonocara stuartgranti "Maulana"

Aquarium　　　Chitimba-Population, Chilumba, Malawi

Aulonocara stuartgranti "Mbenji"

Aquarium　　　Mbenji-Island-Population, Malawi

Aulonocara stuartgranti "Mbenji" ♀

Aquarium　　　Mbenji-Island-Population, Malawi

Aulonocara "Walteri"

Aquarium

Aulonocara "Walteri" ♀

Aquarium

Aulonocara "Walteri"

Aquarium

Aulonocara "Yellow Top"
(= Aulonocara "Lwanda")

　　　Hai Reef, Tanzania

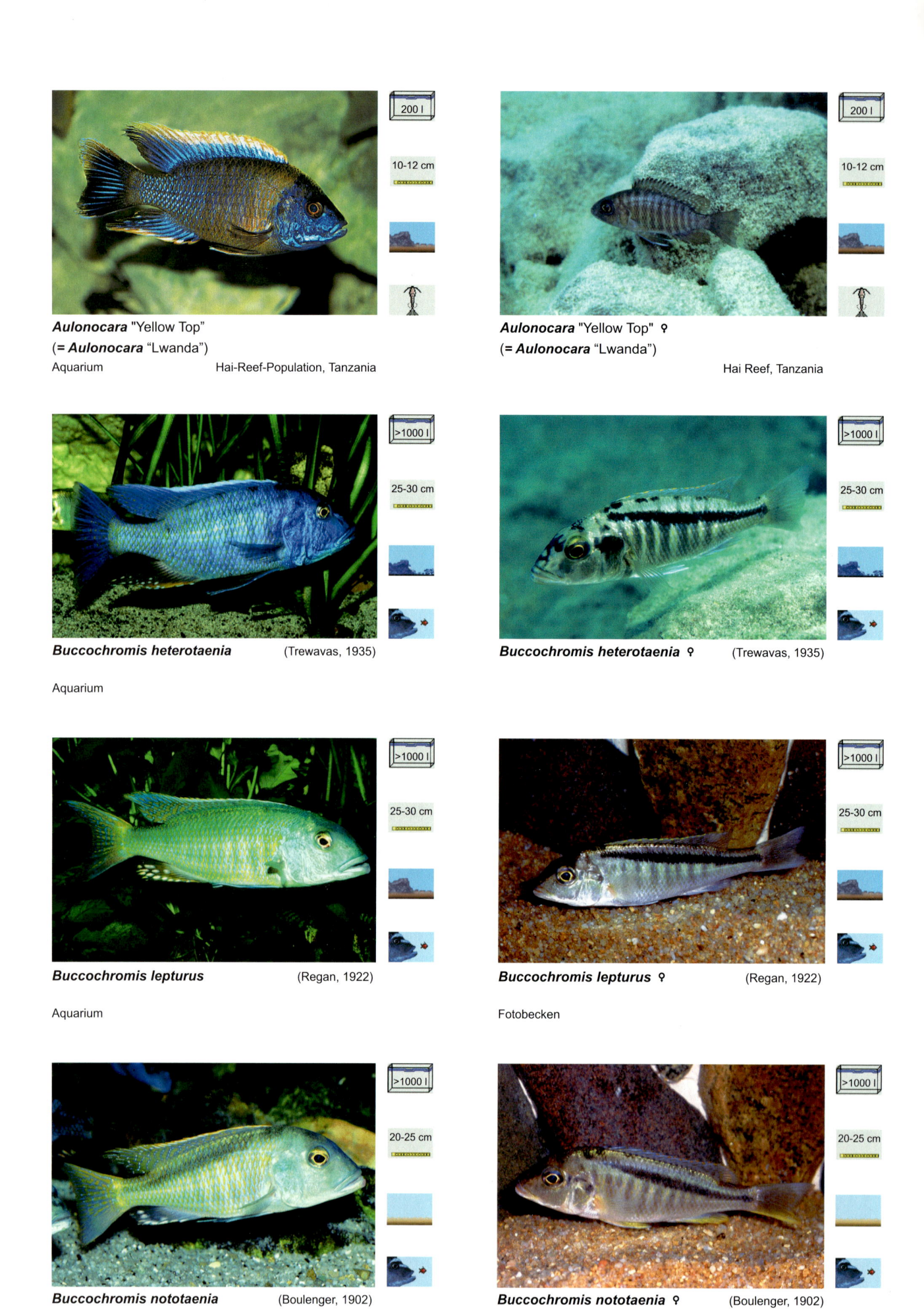

Aulonocara "Yellow Top"
(= **Aulonocara** "Lwanda")

Aquarium   Hai-Reef-Population, Tanzania

Aulonocara "Yellow Top" ♀
(= **Aulonocara** "Lwanda")

                            Hai Reef, Tanzania

Buccochromis heterotaenia   (Trewavas, 1935)

Aquarium

Buccochromis heterotaenia ♀   (Trewavas, 1935)

Buccochromis lepturus   (Regan, 1922)

Aquarium

Buccochromis lepturus ♀   (Regan, 1922)

Fotobecken

Buccochromis nototaenia   (Boulenger, 1902)

Aquarium

Buccochromis nototaenia ♀   (Boulenger, 1902)

Fotobecken

Buccochromis oculatus (Trewavas, 1935)

Likoma-Island, Malawi

Buccochromis rhoadesii (Boulenger, 1908)

Aquarium

Buccochromis rhoadesii ♀ (Boulenger, 1908)

Aquarium

Caprichromis liemi (McKaye & Mackenzie, 1982)

Boadzulu Island, Malawi

Caprichromis orthognathus (Trewavas, 1935)

Eccles Reef, Malawi

Caprichromis orthognathus ♀ (Trewavas, 1935)

Eccles Reef, Malawi

Champsochromis caeruleus (Boulenger, 1908)

Aquarium

Champsochromis caeruleus ♀ (Boulenger, 1908)

Aquarium

Champsochromis spilorhynchus (Regan, 1922)

Aquarium

Champsochromis spilorhynchus ♀ (Regan, 1922)

Fotobecken

Cheilochromis euchilus (Trewavas, 1935)

Aquarium

Cheilochromis euchilus ♀ (Trewavas, 1935)

Chewere/Chilumba, Malawi

Chilotilapia rhoadesii Boulenger, 1908

Aquarium

Chilotilapia rhoadesii ♀ Boulenger, 1908

Aquarium

Copadichromis azureus Konings, 1990

Fotobecken — Mbenji Island, Malawi

Copadichromis azureus Konings, 1990

Aquarium — Maleri-Island-Population, Malawi

Copadichromis borleyi (Iles, 1960)

Mpanga Rocks/Chilumba, Malawi

Copadichromis borleyi (Iles, 1960)

Mara Point/Cobué, Mozambique

Copadichromis borleyi (Iles, 1960)

Fotobecken — Namalenji Island, Malawi

Copadichromis borleyi (Iles, 1960)
(= C. borleyi "Gold Fin")
Fotobecken — Ft. Maguire, Malawi

Copadichromis borleyi (Iles, 1960)
(= C. borleyi "Kadango Red Fin")
Aquarium — Kadango-Population, Malawi

Copadichromis borleyi ♀ (Iles, 1960)
(= C. borleyi "Kadango Red Fin")
Kadango-Population, Malawi

Copadichromis chrysonotus (Boulenger, 1908)

Mazimbwe Island/Likoma-Island, Malawi

Copadichromis chrysonotus ♀ (Boulenger, 1908)

Ngkuyo Island/Mbamba Bay, Tanzania

Copadichromis chrysonotus (Boulenger, 1908)

Aquarium

Copadichromis chrysonotus ♀ (Boulenger, 1908)

Aquarium

Copadichromis cyaneus (Trewavas, 1935)

Fotobecken Mumbo Island, Malawi

Copadichromis cyaneus (Trewavas, 1935)

Mumbo Island, Malawi

Copadichromis "Fire Crest Wimpel"
(= ? Copadichromis virginalis)
Gome Rock/Makanjila, Malawi

Copadichromis "Fire Crest Wimpel"
(= ? Copadichromis virginalis)
Nkanda, Tanzania

Copadichromis geertsi Konings, 1999
(ex: Copadichromis "Fire Crest Blotch"*)*
Gome Rock/Makanjila, Malawi

Copadichromis geertsi ♀ Konings, 1999
(ex: Copadichromis "Fire Crest Blotch")
Gome Rock/Makanjila, Malawi

Copadichromis ilesi   Konings, 1999
(ex: Copadichromis "Fire Crest Yellow")
Nkanda, Tanzania

Copadichromis ilesi   Konings, 1999
(Ex: Copadichromis "Fire Crest Yellow")
Tome Rock/Makanjila, Malawi

Copadichromis jacksoni   (Iles, 1960)
Masinje/Makanjila, Malawi

Copadichromis jacksoni   (Iles, 1960)
Madimba/Likoma Island, Malawi

Copadichromis "Kawanga"
Aquarium   Kawanga-Population, Malawi

Copadichromis "Kawanga" ♀
Aquarium   Kawanga-Population, Malawi

Copadichromis mbenjii   Konings, 1999
Mbenji Island, Malawi

Copadichromis mbenjii ♀   Konings, 1999
Fotobecken   Mbenji Island, Malawi

Copadichromis "Mloto Midnight"

Namisi Rock/Cobue, Mozambique

Copadichromis "Mloto Midnight" ♀

Südl. Mara Point/Cobue, Mozambique

Copadichromis "Mloto Yellow Fin"

Aquarium

Copadichromis "Mloto Yellow Fin" ♀

Aquarium

Copadichromis "Munnae"

Likoma Island, Malawi

Copadichromis "Munnae" ♀

Fotobecken   Likoma Island, Malawi

Copadichromis quadrimaculatus   (Regan, 1922)

Makanjila, Malawi

Copadichromis "Three Spot Eastern"

Nakanthenga Island, Malawi

Copadichromis trewavasae   Konings, 1999
(ex: Copadichromis "Mloto White Top"*)*
Fotobecken   Likoma Island, Malawi

Copadichromis trewavasae   Konings, 1999
(ex: Copadichromis "Mloto White Top"*)*
Lupingu, Tanzania

Copadichromis cf. trimaculatus ♀   (Iles, 1960)
Aquarium

Copadichromis cf. Trimaculatus   (Iles, 1960)
Aquarium

Copadichromis verduyni   Konings, 1990
Aquarium   Makanjila-Population, Malawi

Copadichromis verduyni ♀   Konings, 1990
Makanjila, Malawi

Copadichromis verduyni   Konings, 1990
Fotobecken   Makanjila, Malawi

Copadichromis "Verduyni Blueface"
Nyamizimu/Meponda, Mozambique

Copadichromis "Verduyni Blueface" ♀

Jilambo, Mozambik

Copadichromis "Verduyni Blueface"

Jilambo, Mozambik

Copadichromis "Verduyni Deep Blue" ♀

Kirondo, Tanzania

Copadichromis "Verduyni Deep Blue"

Kirondo, Tanzania

Copadichromis "Verduyni Deep Blue"

Mara Rocks/Mbamba Bay, Tanzania

Copadichromis "Verduyni Deep Blue"

Puulu, Tanzania

Copadichromis "Verduyni Northern"

Nkanda, Tanzania

Copadichromis "Verduyni Northern" ♀

Nkanda, Tanzania

Copadichromis "Verduyni White Blaze"

Ngulu/Chiloelo/Mozambique

Copadichromis "Verduyni White Blaze" ♀

Ngulu/Chiloelo/Mozambique

Copadichromis "Verduyni White Blaze"

Ngulu/Chiloelo/Mozambique

Copadichromis "Verduyni White Blaze"

Ngulu/Chiloelo/Mozambique

Corematodus taeniatus   Trewavas, 1935

Makanjila, Malawi

Corematodus taeniatus   Trewavas, 1935

Aquarium

Ctenopharynx nitidus   (Trewavas, 1935)

N'tekete/Makanjila, Malawi

Ctenopharynx nitidus ♀   (Trewavas, 1935)

Lumbira, Tanzania

Ctenopharynx pictus (Trewavas, 1935)

Chitendi Island/Chilumba, Malawi

Ctenopharynx pictus ♀ (Trewavas, 1935)

Makonde, Tanzania

Cyrtocara moorii Boulenger, 1902

Aquarium

Cyrtocara moorii ♀ Boulenger, 1902

Aquarium

Dimidiochromis compressiceps (Boulenger, 1908)

Aquarium

Dimidiochromis compressiceps ♀ (Boulenger, 1908)

Aquarium

Dimidiochromis kiwinge (Ahl, 1927)

Aquarium

Dimidiochromis kiwinge ♀ (Ahl, 1927)

Likoma-Island, Malawi

Dimidiochromis strigatus (Regan, 1922)

Aquarium

Dimidiochromis strigatus ♀ (Regan, 1922)

Fotobecken

Diplotaxodon argenteus Trewavas, 1935

Makanjila, Malawi

Diplotaxodon greenwoodi Stauffer & McKaye, 1986

Diplotaxodon spec.

Nkhata Bay, Malawi

Diplotaxodon "White Top"

Lwezya Reef/Chitimba, Malawi

Docimodus evelynae Eccles & Lewis, 1976

Docimodus johnstonii Boulenger, 1896

Fotobecken

91

Eclectochromis "Hertae"

Aquarium — Likoma-Island-Population, Malawi

Eclectochromis "Hertae" ♀

Aquarium — Likoma-Island-Population, Malawi

Eclectochromis "Labrosus Mbenji"

Aquarium — Likoma-Island-Population, Malawi

Eclectochromis "Labrosus Mbenji" ♀

Aquarium — Likoma-Island-Population, Malawi

Eclectochromis milomo (Oliver, 1989)

Aquarium

Eclectochromis milomo ♀ (Oliver, 1989)

Aquarium

Eclectochromis ornatus (Oliver, 1989)

Aquarium — Makanjila-Population, Malawi

Eclectochromis ornatus ♀ (Regan, 1922)

Aquarium — Makanjila-Population, Malawi

Exochochromis anagenys ♀ (Oliver, 1989)
Makokola Reef, Malawi

Exochochromis anagenys (Oliver, 1989)
Aquarium

Exochochromis anagenys juv. (Oliver, 1989)
Aquarium

Exochochromis anagenys
Aquarium

Fossorochromis rostratus (Boulenger, 1899)
Aquarium

Fossorochromis rostratus ♀ (Boulenger, 1899)
Aquarium

Fossorochromis rostratus (Boulenger, 1899)
Aquarium

Hemitaeniochromis urotaenia (Regan, 1922)
Aquarium

Hemitilapia oxyrhynchus ♀   Boulenger, 1902

Aquarium   Likoma-Island-Population, Malawi

Hemitilapia oxyrhynchus   Boulenger, 1902

Aquarium   Likoma-Island-Population, Malawi

Lethrinops lethrinus   (Günther, 1893)

Aquarium

Lethrinops "Longipinnis Ntekete"

N´tekete/Makanjila, Malawi

Lethrinops "Makokola" ♀

Aquarium

Lethrinops "Makokola"

Aquarium

Lethrinops cf. oculatus   (Trewavas, 1931)

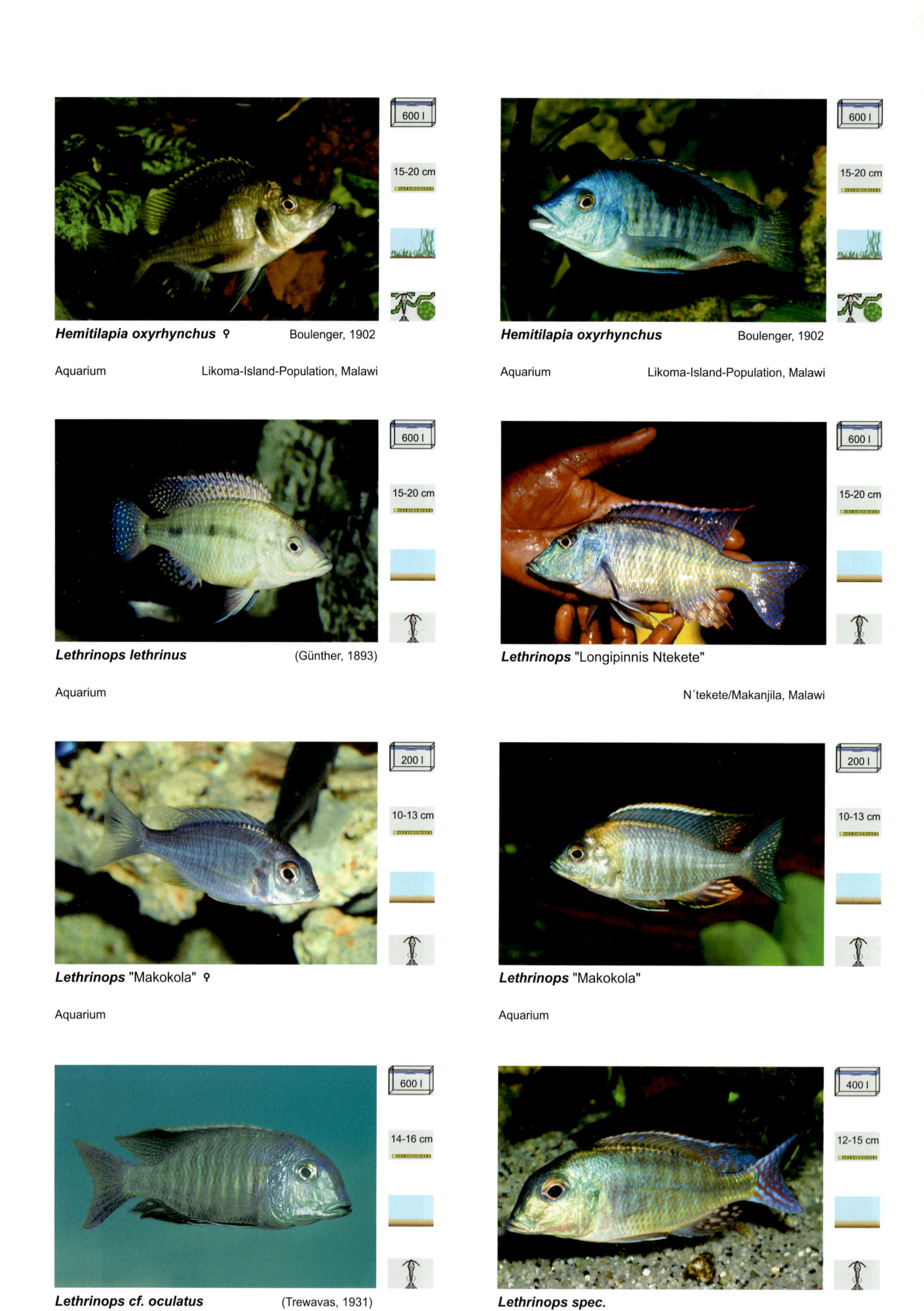

Mphande/Metangula, Mozambique

Lethrinops spec.

Aquarium

Lethrinops "Yellow Collar" ♀

Likoma Island, Malawi

Lethrinops "Yellow Collar"

Likoma Island, Malawi

Lethrinops "Yellow Collar" ♀

Mbamba Bay, Tanzania

Lethrinops "Yellow Collar"

Mbamba Bay, Tanzania

Lichnochromis acuticeps Trewavas, 1935

Aquarium

Lichnochromis acuticeps ♀ Trewavas, 1935

Aquarium

Mylochromis anaphyrmus
(Burgess & Axelrod, 1973)
Namalenji Island, Malawi

Mylochromis anaphyrmus ♀
(Burgess & Axelrod, 1973)
Namalenji Island, Malawi

Mylochromis ensatus   Turner & Howarth, 2001

Aquarium

Mylochromis ensatus ♀   Turner & Howarth, 2001

Senga Bay, Malawi

Mylochromis epichorialis   (Trewavas, 1935)

Aquarium

Mylochromis epichorialis ♀   (Trewavas, 1935)

Mbenji Island, Malawi

Mylochromis ericotaenia   (Regan, 1922)

Aquarium

Mylochromis ericotaenia   (Regan, 1922)

N'tekete/Makanjla, Malawi

Mylochromis ericotaenia   (Regan, 1922)

Aquarium

Mylochromis ericotaenia ♀   (Regan, 1922)

Aquarium

Mylochromis formosus (Trewavas, 1935)
Aquarium

Mylochromis formosus ♀ (Trewavas, 1935)
Aquarium

Mylochromis cf. incola (Trewavas, 1935)
(ex: M. "Golden Mola")
Fotobecken — Maleri Island, Malawi

Mylochromis cf. incola ♀ (Trewavas, 1935)
(ex: M. "Golden Mola")
Fotobecken — Maleri Island, Malawi

Mylochromis cf. incola (Trewavas, 1935)
(ex: M. "Golden Mola")
Maleri Island, Malawi

Mylochromis cf. incola ♀ (Trewavas, 1935)
(ex: M. "Golden Mola")
Maleri Island, Malawi

Mylochromis "Kande"
Kande Island, Malawi

Mylochromis "Kande"
Aquarium — Kande-Island-Population, Malawi

Mylochromis labidodon ♀ (Trewavas, 1935)

Mylochromis labidodon (Trewavas, 1935)

Aquarium

Mylochromis lateristriga ♀ (Günther, 1864)

Aquarium

Mylochromis lateristriga (Günther, 1864)

Aquarium

Mylochromis "Magarettae Stripe" ♀

Fotobecken   Likoma-Island, Malawi

Mylochromis "Magarettae Stripe"

Fotobecken   Likoma-Island, Malawi

Mylochromis "Mchuse"

Aquarium

Mylochromis "Mchuse"

Lupingu, Tanzania

Mylochromis melanotaenia (Regan, 1922)

Aquarium

Mylochromis melanotaenia ♀ (Regan, 1922)

Aquarium

Mylochromis mola (Trewavas, 1935)

Aquarium

Mylochromis mola ♀ (Trewavas, 1935)

Aquarium

Mylochromis "Pointed Head"

Fotobecken　　　　Makanjila, Malawi

Mylochromis "Pointed Head" ♀

Aquarium　　　　Makanjila-Population, Malawi

Mylochromis "Pointed Head"
(ex: M. "Pointed Head Tanzania")

Hai Reef, Tanzania

Mylochromis "Pointed Head" ♀
(ex: M. "Pointed Head Tanzania")

Hai Reef, Tanzania

Mylochromis semipalatus (Trewavas, 1935)

Aquarium

Mylochromis sphaerodon (Regan, 1922)

Aquarium

Naevochromis chrysogaster (Trewavas, 1935)

Aquarium

Naevochromis chrysogaster ♀ (Trewavas, 1935)

Mara Point/Cobué, Mozambique

Nimbochromis fuscotaeniatus (Regan, 1922)

Aquarium

Nimbochromis fuscotaeniatus ♀ (Regan, 1922)

Aquarium

Nimbochromis linni (Burgess & Axelrod, 1975)

Aquarium

Nimbochromis linni ♀ (Burgess & Axelrod, 1975)

Makanjila, Malawi

Nimbochromis livingstonii (Günther, 1893)

Aquarium

Nimbochromis livingstonii (Günther, 1893)

Makanjila, Malawi

Nimbochromis polystigma (Regan, 1922)

Aquarium

Nimbochromis polystigma ♀ (Regan, 1922)

Aquarium

Nimbochromis venustus (Boulenger, 1908)

Aquarium

Nimbochromis venustus ♀ (Boulenger, 1908)

Aquarium

Nyassachromis cf. Microcephalus (Trewavas, 1935)

Makanjila, Malawi

Nyassachromis cf. microcephalus ♀ Trewavas, 1935)

Aquarium

Otopharynx "Blue" ♀

Aquarium

Otopharynx "Blue"

Aquarium

Otopharynx "Blue Yellow Tanzania"

Otopharynx "Blue Yellow Tanzania"

Aquarium

Otopharynx "Blue Yellow Tanzania"

Ngumbe Rock/Minga Bay, Mozambique

Otopharynx cf. *Heterodon* (Trewavas, 1935)

Chilumba, Malawi

Otopharynx lithobates (Oliver, 1989)

Aquarium

Otopharynx lithobates (Oliver, 1989)

Aquarium

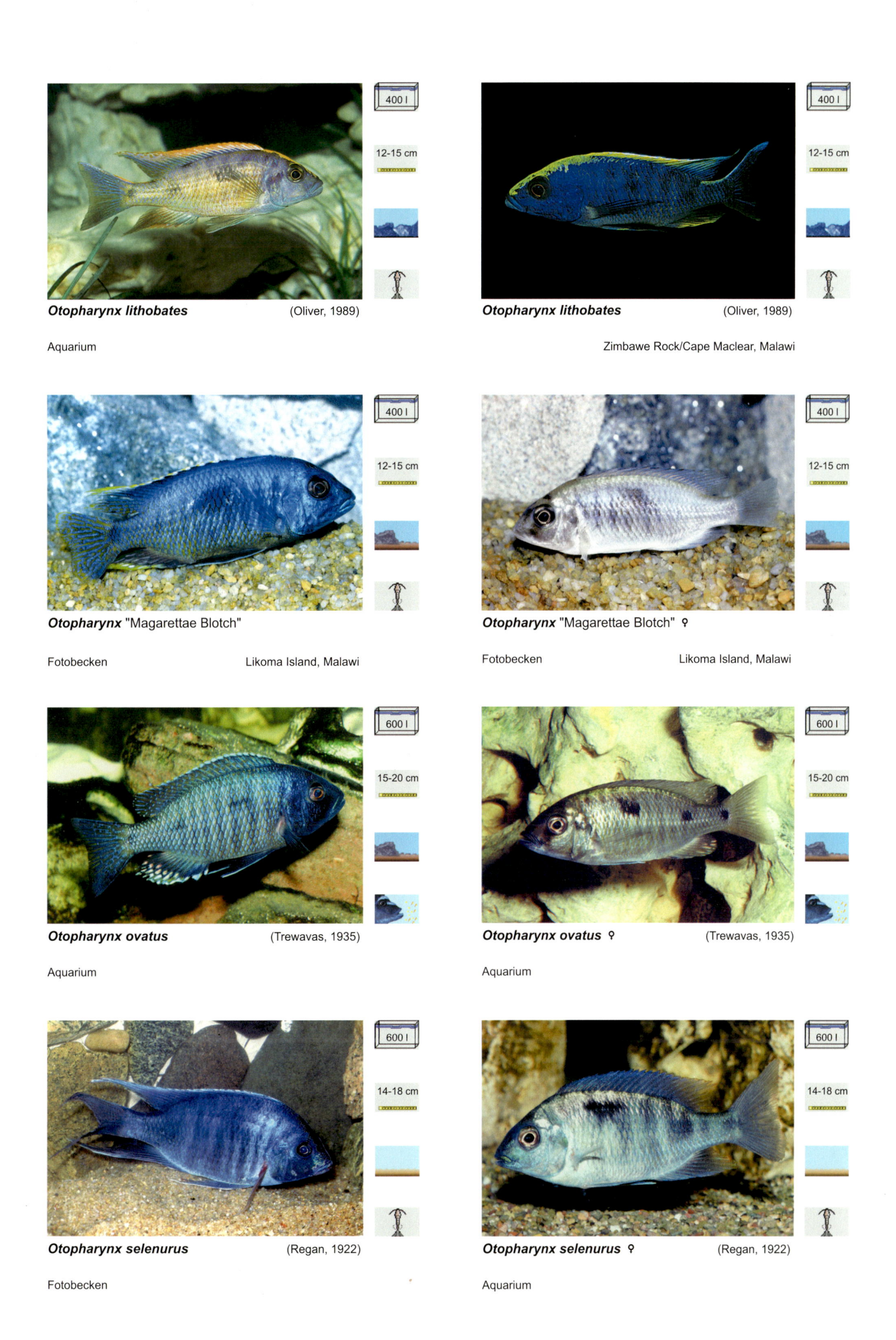

Otopharynx lithobates (Oliver, 1989)

Aquarium

Otopharynx lithobates (Oliver, 1989)

Zimbawe Rock/Cape Maclear, Malawi

Otopharynx "Magarettae Blotch"

Fotobecken   Likoma Island, Malawi

Otopharynx "Magarettae Blotch" ♀

Fotobecken   Likoma Island, Malawi

Otopharynx ovatus (Trewavas, 1935)

Aquarium

Otopharynx ovatus ♀ (Trewavas, 1935)

Aquarium

Otopharynx selenurus (Regan, 1922)

Fotobecken

Otopharynx selenurus ♀ (Regan, 1922)

Aquarium

103

Otopharynx speciosus (Trewavas, 1935)

Likoma Island, Malawi

Otopharynx cf. *Tetrastigma* (Günther, 1893)

Thumbi West Island, Malawi

Otopharynx walteri Konings, 1990

Aquarium

Otopharynx walteri Konings, 1990

Aquarium

Otopharynx walteri Konings, 1990

Maleri Island, Malawi

Pallidochromis tokolosh Turner, 1994

Narungu/Makanjila, Malawi

Placidochromis electra (Burgess, 1983)

Aquarium Likoma-Island-Population, Malawi

Placidochromis electra ♀ (Burgess, 1983)

Aquarium Likoma-Island-Population, Malawi

Placidochromis electra (Burgess, 1983)

N'tekete/Makanjila, Malawi

Placidochromis "Electra Blue Hongi"

Aquarium   Hongi-Island-Population, Tanzania

Placidochromis "Electra Blue Hongi"

Lupono/Mbamba Bay, Tanzania

Placidochromis "Electra Makonde"

Aquarium

Placidochromis "Electra Makonde" ♀

Lupingu, Tanzania

Placidochromis johnstoni (Günther, 1893)

Aquarium

Placidochromis johnstoni ♀ (Günther, 1893)

Aquarium

Placidochromis "Johnstoni Solo"

Kirondo, Tanzania

105

Placidochromis cf. **Phenochilus** (Trewavas, 1935)

Lupingu, Tanzania

Platygnathochromis melanonotus (Regan, 1922)

Aquarium

Protomelas annectens (Regan, 1922)

Aquarium

Protomelas annectens ♀ (Regan, 1922)

Aquarium

Protomelas fenestratus (Trewavas, 1935)

Aquarium

Protomelas fenestratus ♀ (Trewavas, 1935)

Likoma Island, Malawi

Protomelas "Fenestratus Ngkuyo"

Aquarium   Ngkuyo-Island-Population/Mbamba Bay, Tanzania

Protomelas "Fenestratus Ngkuyo" ♀

Aquarium   Ngkuyo-Island-Population/Mbamba Bay, Tanzania

Protomelas "Fenestratus Taiwan"

Taiwan Reef/Chisumulu Island, Malawi

Protomelas "Fenestratus Taiwan" ♀

Taiwan Reef/Chisumulu Island, Malawi

Protomelas insignis (Trewavas, 1935)

Aquarium

Protomelas insignis ♀ (Trewavas, 1935)

Aquarium

Protomelas labridens (Trewavas, 1935)

Protomelas labridens ♀ (Trewavas, 1935)

Aquarium

Protomelas similis (Regan, 1922)

Likoma Island, Malawi

Protomelas similis ♀ (Regan, 1922)

Fotobecken Likoma Island, Malawi

Protomelas spilonotus (Trewavas, 1935)

Aquarium — Mbenji-Island-Population, Malawi

Protomelas spilonotus ♀ (Trewavas, 1935)

Aquarium — Mbenji-Island-Population, Malawi

Protomelas "Spilonotus Mozambique"

Aquarium

Protomelas "Spilonotus Tanzania"

Aquarium

Protomelas "Spilonotus Tanzania" ♀

Aquarium

Protomelas spilopterus (Trewavas, 1935)

Fotobecken

Protomelas spilopterus ♀ (Trewavas, 1935)

Aquarium

Protomelas "Spilopterus Blue"

Ifungu/Livingstone-Mountains, Tanzania

Protomelas "Spiloptenus Blue" ♀

Tumbi Reef, Tanzania

Protomelas taeniolatus (Trewavas, 1935)

Fotobecken

Protomelas taeniolatus (Trewavas, 1935)

Aquarium Namalenji-Island-Population, Malawi

Protomelas taeniolatus ♀ (Trewavas, 1935)

Aquarium Namalenji-Island-Population, Malawi

Protomelas taeniolatus (Trewavas, 1935)

Mbenji Island, Malawi

Rhamphochromis esox (Boulenger, 1908)

Aquarium

Rhamphochromis spec.

Senga Bay, Malawi

Rhamphochromis spec.

Liuli, Tanzania

109

Sciaenochromis fryeri Konings, 1993

Aquarium

Sciaenochromis fryeri Konings, 1993

Aquarium

Sciaenochromis gracilis (Trewavas, 1935)

Aquarium

Sciaenochromis gracilis ♀ (Trewavas, 1935)

Aquarium

Sciaenochromis psammophilus Konings, 1993

Aquarium

Sciaenochromis spec.

Aquarium

Sciaenochromis spilostichus (Trewavas, 1935)

Aquarium

Stigmatochromis "Cave"

Makanjila, Malawi

110

Stigmatochromis modestus (Günther, 1893)

Aquarium

Stigmatochromis modestus ♀ (Günther, 1893)

Aquarium

Stigmatochromis "Modestus Eastern"

Aquarium Makanjila-Population, Malawi

Stigmatochromis pholidophorus (Trewavas, 1935)

Aquarium

Stigmatochromis pholidophorus (Trewavas, 1935)

Aquarium

Stigmatochromis "Tolae"

Aquarium

Stigmatochromis woodi (Regan, 1922)

Aquarium

Stigmatochromis woodi ♀ (Regan, 1922)

Aquarium

Taeniochromis holotaenia (Regan, 1922)

Aquarium

Taeniochromis holotaenia ♀ (Regan, 1922)

Taeniolethrinops "Black Fin"

Taeniolethrinops "Black Fin"

Taeniolethrinops "Furcicauda Ntekete"

N'tekete/Makanjila, Malawi

Taeniolethrinops cf. *Laticeps* (Trewavas, 1931)

Aquarium

Taeniolethrinops praeorbitalis (Regan, 1922)

Aquarium

Taeniolethrinops praeorbitalis ♀ (Regan, 1922)

Aquarium

Tramitichromis brevis (Boulenger, 1908)

Trematocranus microstoma Trewavas, 1935

Aquarium

Trematocranus placodon (Regan, 1922)

Aquarium

Trematocranus placodon ♀ (Regan, 1922)

Likoma Island, Malawi

Tyrannochromis macrostoma (Regan, 1922)

Tyrannochromis macrostoma ♀ (Regan, 1922)

Aquarium

Tyrannochromis nigriventer Eccles, 1989

Aquarium   Chilumba-Population, Malawi

Tyrannochromis nigriventer ♀ Eccles, 1989

Aquarium   Chilumba-Population, Malawi

113

Tyrannochromis nigriventer　　　Eccles, 1989

Chinyamwezi Island, Malawi

Tyrannochromis nigriventer　　　Eccles, 1989

Aquarium　　　Chilumba-Population, Malawi

Astatotilapia calliptera　　　(Günther, 1883)

Aquarium

Astatotilapia calliptera ♀　　　(Günther, 1883)

Aquarium

Oreochromis spec.

Likoma Island, Malawi

Oreochromis spec.

Likoma Island, Malawi

Serranochromis robustus robustus　(Günther, 1864)

Fotobecken

Tilapia rendalli　　　Boulenger, 1896

Aquarium

FEMANGA®

http://www.femanga.de

Der natürlichere Weg zum gesunden Aquarium!

Tel. 0208 – 449056   Fax 0208 – 449066
e-mail: info@femanga.de

Erläuterung zu den Symbolen

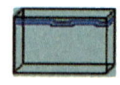

Aquariengröße

Hierbei handelt es sich um empfohlene Beckengrößen, wobei von einer üblichen Beckenform (Länge x Tiefe x Höhe: z. B. 170 cm x 60 cm x 60 cm = 612 Liter Inhalt) ausgegangen wurde. Die Beckengrößen wurden in abgestufter Form festgelegt: 200 l = kleines Malawisee-Becken; 400 l = mittelgroßes Becken; 600 l = großes Becken; 1000 l = sehr großes Becken; > 1000 l = Spezialbecken).
Die Angaben gelten für Gemeinschaftsbecken, in denen üblicherweise mehrere Arten von Malawisee-Cichliden miteinander vergesellschaftet werden. Viele Malawisee-Cichliden können aber auch in Artenbecken gepflegt und gezüchtet werden, die deutlich kleiner sind als die hier empfohlenen Becken.

Weiterhin gilt, daß sich die Beckengrößen-Empfehlung auf ausgewachsene, durchschnittlich große Exemplare bezieht. Manche Arten werden im Handel aber überwiegend als Jungtiere oder Halbwüchsige angeboten. Z. B. werden Wildfänge von Dimidiochromis kiwinge meist in einer Größe von ca. 10 cm eingeführt, die Endgröße liegt aber bei über 30 cm. Da diese Art sehr schwimmfreudig und auch sehr durchsetzungsfähig ist, wird konsequenterweise ein Becken von über 1000 l empfohlen. Gleichwohl ist es selbstverständlich möglich, halbwüchsige Exemplare über eine sehr lange Zeit z. B. in einem 600 l Aquarium zu pflegen, bis sie eine Größe erreicht haben, die eine Überführung in ein größeres Becken zwingend erfordert.

Gesamtlänge

Der hier in Zentimetern angegebene Größenbereich bezieht sich auf die Gesamtlänge (Körperlänge mit Schwanzflosse) der abgebildeten Art, unabhängig von der Gesamtlänge des abgebildeten Exemplars. Es ist zu betonen, das dieser Größenbereich sowohl unter- als auch überschritten werden kann. Insbesondere die Mbunas können im Aquarium bei reichlicher Fütterung sehr viel größer als im See werden. Beispielsweise sind Labidochromis-Wildfänge meist nur etwa 6-8 cm groß; im Aquarium erreichen diese Arten aber deutlich über 10 cm, manchmal auch 12 cm. Pseudotropheus-Arten, die üblicherweise 10-12 cm groß werden, sind im Aquarium mitunter über 15 cm lang. Umgekehrt ist es bei vielen großwerdenden Nicht-Mbunas. Tyrannochromis macrostoma erreicht im Malawisee häufig Längen von über 25 cm. Im Aquarium aufgezogene Exemplare bleiben meist kleiner, es sei denn, man hat ein sehr großes Becken (z. B. 2000 l) zur Verfügung. Um all diesen Umständen wenigstens annähernd Rechnung zu tragen, wurden keine maximalen Endgrößen, sondern ein entsprechender Größenbereich angegeben, in dem die meisten Exemplaren einer jeweiligen Art unter natürlichen Bedingungen liegen.

Ernährung

- Aufwuchs
- Kleintiere
- Eier/Larven
- Plankton
- Fische
- Flossen/Schuppen

Alle Angaben zur Ernährung beziehen sich auf das natürliche Beutespektrum im Malawisee. Im Aquarium fressen fast alle Arten fast alles. Bei den Mbunas wurde nahezu durchgängig das Symbol „Aufwuchsfresser" verwandt. Unberücksichtigt blieb hier also, daß sich viele Mbunas zu Zeiten der Planktonblüte überwiegend von planktischen Organismen ernähren und dabei den Aufwuchs weitgehend verschmähen. Als „Kleintierfresser" wurden diejenigen Arten bezeichnet, die relativ unspezialisiert alles fressen und auch mal einen kleinen Fisch erbeuten. Arten, die sich überwiegend von anderen Fischen ernähren, erhielten das Symbol „Fischfresser".
Spezialanpassungen bilden die „Flossen- und Schuppenfresser" sowie die sogenannten „pädophagen" Cichliden. Letztere haben sich offensichtlich darauf spezialisiert, maulbrütende Weibchen inbesondere im Maulbereich zu attakkieren mit dem Ziel, ein Freisetzen der Brut zu erreichen.

Lebensraum

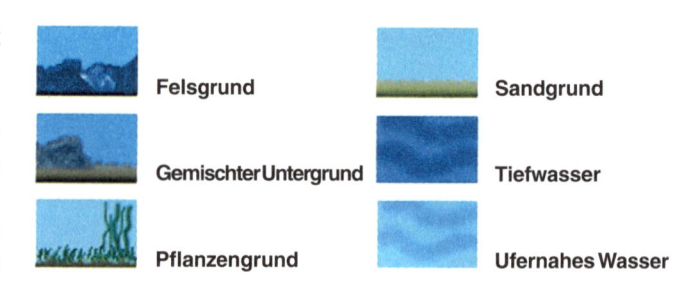

- Felsgrund
- Gemischter Untergrund
- Pflanzengrund
- Sandgrund
- Tiefwasser
- Ufernahes Wasser

Analog zum Symbol „Ernährung" beziehen sich die Angaben zum Lebensraum nur auf natürliche Verhältnisse. Unterschieden wird nach felsigen (= steinigen), sandigen und gemischten (Sand-Fels) Untergründen. Eine Differenzierung nach Fels- und Steingrund erfolgte nicht. Weiterhin sind mit Pflanzen bewachsene Bereiche als „Pflanzengrund" aufgeführt. Ein weiterer Lebensraum ist das „Freiwasser", wobei damit hier nur das ufernahe Freiwasser gemeint ist. Tiefwasserbewohner sind mit einem gesonderten Symbol gekennzeichnet; Angaben zum Untergrund in tiefem Wasser sind bislang kaum bekanntgeworden, vermutlich überwiegt überall im tiefen Wasser schlammig-sandiger Boden.